Maximum Impact

PRAISE FOR *MAXIMUM IMPACT*

"The most important aspect of Board/Superintendent communication is that it must be clear, concise, and factual, with no surprises. The relationship between both parties is predicated on effective communication that builds mutual trust and respect of each other's roles and responsibilities. *Maximum Impact: Boards of Education and Superintendents Communicating as a Team* addresses the Key Works of school leaders."

C. H. "Sonny" Savoie
former president of the National School Boards Association,
current member of St. Charles Parrish Board of Education,
Luling, Louisiana since 1984

"*Maximum Impact* crystallizes an aspect of effective school district governance that every school board member needs to understand: purposeful and strategic communication from district leaders like them is absolutely essential to keeping public education strong in our communities, states, and nation. Making this an even more important read—for new and veteran board members alike—are the practical tips and strategies infused throughout."

Tracey Benson
associate executive director, Arizona School Boards Association,
former chair, Council of School Boards Association Communicators

Maximum Impact

Boards of Education and Superintendents Communicating as a Team

Brian Creasman
and Brad Hughes

ROWMAN & LITTLEFIELD
Lanham • Boulder • New York • London

Published by Rowman & Littlefield
An imprint of The Rowman & Littlefield Publishing Group, Inc.
4501 Forbes Boulevard, Suite 200, Lanham, Maryland 20706
www.rowman.com

6 Tinworth Street, London SE11 5AL, United Kingdom

Copyright © 2020 by Brian Creasman and Brad Hughes

All rights reserved. No part of this book may be reproduced in any form or by any electronic or mechanical means, including information storage and retrieval systems, without written permission from the publisher, except by a reviewer who may quote passages in a review.

British Library Cataloguing in Publication Information Available

Library of Congress Cataloging-in-Publication Data Available

ISBN 978-1-4758-5891-4 (cloth)
ISBN 978-1-4758-5892-1 (pbk.)
ISBN 978-1-4758-5893-8 (electronic)

Contents

Foreword by C. Ed Massey — vii

Opening Testimonial — xi

Introduction: Communication, Collaboration, and COVID-19 — 1

1. Communicating as a Purpose-Driven Team — 5
2. The Importance of "We" not "Me" — 9
3. Communicating When Leaders Differ — 13
4. Board Meetings and Messages — 19
5. Taking Families from Informed to Engaged — 25
6. Two-Way Communicating via the News Media — 31
7. Know When to Talk and Know When to Hold Back — 39
8. Learning and Practicing the Art of Listening — 45
9. Socially Speaking: Online Engagement Matters — 49
10. Putting the Forward Focus on Growth — 55
11. Building and Maintaining Support for Schools — 59
12. Success: See It, Speak It — 65
13. Communicating in a Timely Manner in Calm and in Crisis — 71
14. Mistakes Happen, and How We Acknowledge Them Matters — 77

15 Crafting a Year-Round School Communications Calendar   81

Conclusion : A Final Thought   87

Afterword: Putting *Maximum Impact* into Action by Lisa Bartusek   89

Index   91

About the Authors   93

Foreword

Communication is leadership! In today's ever-changing educational world, communication is vitally important. Communication between board members, between superintendents and board members, between superintendents and the community, and between the board of education and the community is key to advancing achievement in America's schools.

The topic of communication takes many forms, including verbal, nonverbal, and written communication (such as news reports, publications, and social media). This book provides an in-depth look at how communication can cause a district to thrive or cause a district to implode in the fast-paced world in which we operate. Having served first as a substitute teacher and then as a board member for more than 22 years, I have come to understand the significance of communication.

In my time as board member, I moved from printed communications to electronic communications, which includes today's array of social media options. Despite the platform, the underlying principles are the same. Clear communication is key to building relationships between personnel, with the public, and with the media. For schools to advance their message, it must be concise, clear, and captivating.

In the school district where I served, our consistent message was that every student will be college, career, and life ready when they graduate. All other messages are developed around that mission statement. This affected communication with the superintendent, the staff, and the community. It also colors any comments made to the media. By controlling the messaging, the district has established in this concise phrase the objective that drives all actions.

In *Maximum Impact*, the authors will explain how to create a message, control the message, disseminate the message, and adapt the message that drives a district's purpose. The expert information explains how to advance objectives and avoid pitfalls related to communication. Education has been under attack by those who believe their message will resonate with communities better than the message delivered in our existing schools.

Many districts, absent a communication plan, react rather than respond to these seemingly incessant attacks from a defensive position. Too many districts fail to celebrate their successes through positive messaging. This book will guide school leaders and districts to promote the positive and respond positively to the negative messages that are inevitable in the current educational environment.

In reading the chapters of *Maximum Impact* to prepare this foreword, I recalled an incident in Boone County where some community members wanted to arm teachers in response to a recent school shooting elsewhere. The board was inundated with letters, e-mails, and texts demanding we accept this program. Some even called for the removal of all board members who did not support the program.

Instead of reacting, our board responded. We did not initially respond with anything other than a promise to investigate what was in the best interests of the Boone County district. The board followed many of the practices set forth in this book. We listened, investigated, and developed a positive message rather than making a reactionary response.

Communication among the superintendent, board members, administrators, parents, students, and the media was essential to handling this situation. Clear communication with the members of the community and the media allowed our board to navigate a very challenging time. In the end, we elected to implement an already solid emergency plan rather than arm teachers. Only by effective communication and dissemination of information was this response possible. All board members subsequently won reelection, and Boone County continued its course of ensuring every student is college, career, and life ready despite external distractions.

To effectively communicate and maximize the impact of that communication, there must be a plan. Many situations can be expected; however, many cannot. This is especially true given the many threats to schools today, including physical threats and social media threats. The mantra of the Navy Seals is to prepare for the expected and train for the unexpected.

This book will show readers how to create a communication plan, implement the plan, and adapt the plan to the needs of the district. The subjects include dealing with the media, communicating with the community, handling a crisis, promoting the needs of a district, defending the need for equitable and adequate funding, and communicating through the board agenda and social media platforms.

Both authors of *Maximum Impact* are experienced in the subject matter covered herein, and they offer incredible insight on a subject so often disregarded. By utilizing the information in this book, the reader can become a better leader, and the district and the community will benefit as well. *Maximum Impact* is a book that should be read by every school administrator and board member who desires to have a positive impact in the important work of investing in the lives of students and communities.

C. Ed Massey

C. Ed Massey is an attorney and state representative in the Kentucky General Assembly representing the 66th House district. During more than two decades on the Boone County Board of Education, Massey was elected to the Kentucky School Boards Association Board of Directors and the National School Boards Association Board of Directors, and he served as president of both associations. In addition to his law practice, Massey speaks around the country about educational leadership.

Opening Testimonial

Research into what makes a high-performing school board, such as National School Boards Association's "Key Works of School Boards" or the Iowa Lighthouse Inquiry, *always* refers to communication as a key component of successful board leadership. As a Lighthouse trainer, I've studied how to help boards use communication to better their decision-making abilities and to better communicate the district's work to the public. For the district to prosper, this work *must* be successful.

Knowing the authors' expertise in communications I expected a worldly, expertly written guide to communicating to the public, and it is all of that. In particular, the chapter on dealing with the media is full of practical information that only experts on press relations could have written. They know the material but, more importantly, know how to share this wisdom in a way that is easily comprehended.

What I didn't expect was that this book would be so much more. It is a guide into how boards and superintendents can more effectively use communication to be better leaders. It can help board members (and superintendents) develop strategies to make better decisions and to implement them in a way that there is more ownership by the rest of the community. It is full of practical advice on how to be a better leadership team. For school board members (and others) looking to find reading material that can help them better understand how to be effective leaders, this book should be on the short pile.

Nick Caruso
Senior Staff Associate for Field Service and Coordinator of Technology
Connecticut Association of Boards of Education

Introduction

Communication, Collaboration, and COVID-19

America's public schools approaching the third decade of the 21st century face rising complexities: Rising shortages of teachers and administrators. Challenges of a steadily diversifying student body. Stagnant funding while expenses grow. More political activity in development of accountability models. (By the way, politics and education rarely produce learning outcomes that are student-centered rather than adult centered in design.) As pressures mount, the need for local boards of education and superintendents to be strategic in their governance and leadership becomes even more critical.

Often, boards of education and superintendents, paralyzed by inability to combat sudden or systemic changes, fail to recognize that their most powerful tool is communication. A comment that is typical among many school board members and superintendents is, "if only we had communicated to the public better or earlier." This saying brings into focus the importance of communication in public education and the realm of district governance.

Though some may argue whether "culture trumps strategy" or "strategy is more important than culture," we contend communication is the most critical component to culture and strategy. It is all the more reason that boards of education and superintendents must maximize their communication strategies and practices. Communication opens and closes doors—depending on the level of effectiveness. Without question, we conclude that no organization can have an effective culture or strategy without an effective communication strategy.

Communication is the glue that holds strategy and culture together. Think about it: if a superintendent or member of the board of education cannot communicate the district's strategy, does a strategy, in fact, really exist? Likewise, if the district lacks an effective communication strategy, how can a district have a positive organizational culture? A common mistake is that leaders and boards of education assume that communication happened.

We would argue—based on our firsthand experiences; countless trainings; and conversations with board members, superintendents, and others—that without communication a strategy does not exist and a positive culture is somewhat lacking.

We emphasize communication in this era of increasing scrutiny of public education as a tool to help change public perception of public education. Boards of education and superintendents, now more than ever before, must grasp the importance of a strategic and concise communication strategy. School districts must become more proactive and less reactive when it comes to communication.

There needs to be a tidal wave of positive information, news, and images of what is occurring in public education. People react positively to slogans like "We ♥ Public Education." We believe that there must be more, including a regular, intentional focus on communication. This begins with a clear vision and a reimaging of school districts through transparency, concise messages, and a consistent presence in the community.

Some may question whether boards of education and superintendents can have a consistent presence in the community through communication. We enthusiastically believe it can be achieved. As an example of this line of thinking, consider President Franklin Roosevelt's use of radio "fireside chats" to transform the country on the brink of collapse due to the Great Depression.

President Roosevelt maximized communication to the point that citizens all across the country—many of them bankrupt, homeless, and starving—felt energized and connected, not only with Roosevelt but also to the united, national effort. A number of Americans who lived through the Great Depression said that they felt like they knew Roosevelt personally, despite never having met him. FDR understood that proactive communication not only could mobilize people to do impossible things but also enable them to see the positives that existed within a time of many negatives.

Throughout this book, we encourage boards of education and superintendents to change the conversation, to begin a revolution, and to produce positive outcomes for students. Clear, united, and concise communication strategies can actively engage district stakeholders. Though board members and superintendents face a very lonely job, communication can help reduce or eliminate accessibility issues that often lead to a sense of confinement.

Members of the community need to hear from board members and superintendents regularly, outside of the normal release of board meeting minutes. It is not enough to rely on the occasional press release, the chanced news article in the local newspaper, or the sporadic social media post that highlights an event, issue, or positive headline in the school district. A communication strategy with a maximum impact is consistent in message and regular in delivery to targeted audiences.

Effective, steady communication helps boards of education and superintendents define the district. In other cases, school leaders have utilized a consistent message to redefine, transform, and market their districts to prospective teachers, staff members, parents, businesses, and the larger school community. Those particular districts (some may say high-performing districts) enjoy strong public and community support. Why? Because constituents, employees, parents, employers, and students feel that they are informed and empowered by access to information.

We introduce *Maximum Impact* to school board members and superintendents as a guide to help emphasize the importance of communication in their roles as school leaders. Our purpose is to help inform school leaders through a guide with practical strategies, suggestions, and examples. If your school district has a communication strategy that you feel is effective, *Maximum Impact* can be an asset in further strengthening those practices.

If your district is struggling to effectively communicate or to maintain a unified voice or message, then we would encourage the approaches we recommend in our book. Don't become the board of education or superintendent of a district of too many voices, too many visions, collectively leading to too many destinations.

When we began collaborating in early 2019 to produce *Maximum Impact*, neither of us—nor, we assume, most of our readers—knew the terms "coronavirus," "COVID-19," or probably even "pandemic." Today, virtually every significant decision made by school board members and superintendents is influenced—and many are driven—by the changing consequences of the virus in their districts, their communities, their states, and our nation.

Though many view COVID-19 as a medical emergency, which it is, it is also a communication and leadership emergency. In recent history few events, besides those of September 11, 2001, have required superintendents and boards of education to communicate at such a fast pace and with such a sense of urgency. Overnight, superintendents and boards of education that once would be considered quiet transformed into communication hubs—composing communications to be delivered to teachers, staff, families, and community using a variety of mediums based on new information that seemed to be updated every minute.

As *Maximum Impact* was moving closer to final publication, we began to examine whether there were aspects of advice we could include relative to effective school leadership communications strategies and the response to COVID-19. To our delight, we found that much of this book can be applied directly to engaging school stakeholders as much during a pandemic as during times of less dramatic challenges.

For example:

- Objective: School leaders need to explain and educate parents, employees, students, and the general public about COVID-19 instructional as well as health and safety decisions. Chapter 5 is about ensuring that the "informed" school family also is an "engaged" school family.
- Objective: Parents have concerns about sending their children to in-person classes while employees worry about viral exposure and their own health. Leadership responses must begin with understanding those concerns—hence, chapter 8 on the art of listening.
- Objective: A child or an employee tests positive for COVID-19, leading parents and co-workers to demand both information and action. Chapter 13 addresses timely communications best practices that work during a crisis.
- Objective: Critics are questioning, if not directly challenging, school leaders' decisions on any number of coronavirus-related subjects. Often these voices manifest themselves online. Chapter 9 provides leaders with ways to use social media as a tool to explain and engage.
- Objective: Schools need additional resources to meet the different demands of education during the pandemic (masks, thermometers, technology, or additional staff). In chapter 11, we discuss building and maintaining support, including the fiscal bottom line.
- Objective: Aforementioned masks sparked division in numerous school communities around the nation. But our medical experts list masks among the top tools to fight the virus. Chapter 2 offers ideas on communicating about "we" not "me" in dealing with the virus.
- Objective: When a major change affects students or staff—altering the calendar, shifting to online-only instruction, providing meals under new guidance—the news media is an essential partner in informing the public, as spelled out in chapter 6 on ideas about media relations.
- Objective: Schools are nearing the end of the academic year and many positive things have been achieved, made possible by decisions leaders made in preparing for and adapting to COVID-19 matters. In chapter 12, we encourage ways to share those success stories.

In fact, we are convinced that there are potential coronavirus-connected communications strategies that could be gleaned from virtually every chapter in *Maximum Impact*. While they weren't conceived for such challenging times as school boards and superintendents live in—dealing regularly with the virus and its impact on teaching and learning, planning and implementing, managing and modifying—the tenets of effective communications spelled out herein can bolster school leaders' messaging as much in these historic times as when the focus can return to Job 1—ensuring the quality education of every child in every one of your classrooms.

Chapter One

Communicating as a Purpose-Driven Team

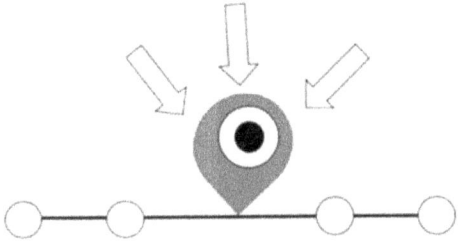

The school board and superintendent team share more than a single goal of supporting student achievement. They also have a common role in informing and educating their stakeholders.

Collaboration and teamwork are vital cogs in the success of any organization. In public schools, this starts at the top—with the board of education (elected or appointed) and the superintendent. This is where governance and leadership mesh together to provide a district's vision, resources, and policies. How effectively each board/superintendent team communicates—internally, externally, officially, personally, individually, and collectively—can have a huge impact (a maximum impact, if you will) on how well various audiences grasp the achievements, challenges, and opportunities in their schools.

Before a board member or superintendent begins reviewing the strategies and techniques that are provided in the pages that follow, they must first understand the purpose of the team. The team we speak of now, and will repeatedly throughout *Maximum Impact*, is the board of education and the superintendent. Each board member and the superintendent form an essential team that is found in every public school district across the nation.

Though the makeup, organizational structure of the board, powers, and roles differ depending on state statutes, there is always a board of education and always a superintendent. The formation and creation of the board of education and the role of superintendent at the beginning of what now is the public education system was meant to empower a group of individuals to make decisions collectively—based on local interests, values, and goals.

Hence, the term "local control" has risen in importance when it comes to education. Statewide and national leaders continue to emphasize local control even though "local control" is not the same as it was when boards of education and the superintendent position were created. The board and superintendent form a team with the expectation to govern and lead the development of a strategic education system in school districts across the United States. Truth be told—all education issues at the end of the day are local.

Enough with background information; you have enough to get going. The important concept that we want to emphasize in this chapter is collaboration and teamwork. The board of education and the superintendent are connected, depending on which state, directly or indirectly. This is where governance and leadership mesh together to form an essential structure that provides vision, resources, supports, and policies for the school organization. In other words, this is where the rubber meets the road—when it comes to governance and leadership in a school district.

The board of education, working closely with the superintendent, democratizes education. Boards of education and superintendents ensure that every student has free access and opportunities in a world full of inequities that often plague communities, neighborhoods, and unfortunately many school districts. The focus on the right to a free education must be emphasized and embossed in the conversation when it comes to boards of education and superintendents.

Ensuring free access and opportunities cannot be accomplished by the work of one board member or the superintendent. As budgets remain stagnant in education, "free" access to learning continues to be challenged and jeopardized. These challenging times are putting more pressures on boards of education and superintendents to think about budgets differently, access differently, through a collaborative lens.

As a team, the board of education and superintendent create an advocacy team—with the sole purpose of advocating for students. This is where a lot of times boards of education and the superintendent derail—as they lose their purpose, they become engaged and entrapped in futile arguments, disagreements, and agenda items.

There must be a clear discussion from the beginning between board members and the superintendent about their moral calling to be educational advocates on a mission to create the best learning experiences, opportunities, and outcomes for every student. This can only be accomplished if the board and superintendent are all rowing in the same direction.

As boards of education and superintendents begin to work together, remaining aligned to their purpose and focused on students, their relationship is strengthened through open and transparent communication. The purpose is solidified through those daily conversations among board members, among board members and the superintendent, and among the board of education, the superintendent, and the general public.

Communication helps resonate "team" throughout the school organization and the community. Communication makes governance and leadership personal—tearing down job titles and roles—and helps make each member of the board and the superintendent feel they are a part of the team and essential to the mission to help create change in the district and help every student succeed.

Furthermore, communication helps reinforce the purpose of the board. When disagreements occur, which happens within the most effective and high-performing boards of education and school districts, the team's history of communicating will either help the team refocus on the purpose quickly or derail. Effective communication doesn't occur overnight; instead, it is a process that requires daily practice.

Members of the board and the superintendent must work together to find the best way to communicate with each other and within the team and remain purpose driven, instead of having to focus on disagreements that will prevent the district from moving forward. Only by working together as a team can the district continue to meet the diverse needs of students. Today's schools need an effective board of education and superintendent team that focuses on issues that matter—not the minuscule issues that have nothing to do with the success of the student.

Members of the board of education and the superintendent must never lose focus on their purpose. Each member of the team is important to creating change that will result in success for each student. Like other teams and organizations, the board of education and superintendent will only be as effective as the weakest team member—which is why continuous learning, training, interactions, and communication will help strengthen each team member, thus making their purpose not only to become more focused but also to spread throughout the school district and community.

Few things are invariably as powerful as a purpose-driven team, where every team member not only knows their role, feels valued, is comfortable providing input, is open to criticism, and is willing to own failure but also shares successes. But these purpose-driven teams only occur if there is a team culture where communication is present—where listening is just as important as speaking. Teams are too quick to speak and miss the opportunity to listen. Teams grow by listening to each other and the people they serve.

PRACTICAL STRATEGIES

- *Grow, grow, grow.* Board members and the superintendent need to continually seek opportunities to grow individually and as a team. Ongoing learning (growing) only strengthens a purpose-driven team. Never stop, as the minute the team rests, complacency will swoop in and begin to dismantle the team's purpose *and* commodore.
- *Be open to change.* Though the purpose of the board of education and the superintendent is always students, change will inevitably need to occur. As students continue to diversify, their needs, goals, and aspirations will change. As students change, the board of education and superintendent will need to work together to ensure that their purpose remains relevant to student-centered needs and goals.
- *Take the time to communicate and model the team's purpose.* The best way to stay on message is to continually communicate the board's, superintendent's, and the team's purpose. Think about starting every board meeting with communicating the team's purpose—in simple terms—to board members, the superintendent, and guests. Why is each team member there? Why did each want to be a board member, the superintendent, or a part of the team? Publicly talking about the purpose is one of the ways (there are several others) to help model the team's agenda, calling for a laser focus on students.

KEY TAKEAWAY

Never forget the team's purpose. To help the board of education and the superintendent remain focused, communicate the team's purpose regularly and consistently. There is no better way to help the team remain focused and everyone else to understand the team's focus than by communicating the purpose proudly. Focus on team—and not individual—agendas. Individual agendas will become obstacles not only to the team's mission and vision for the school district but also, ultimately, will be catastrophic to the communication strategy. A dysfunctional team cannot communicate effectively.

Chapter Two

The Importance of "We" not "Me"

Board of Education with "W" underlined above
Superintendent with "M" underlined and circled with a slash through it

Of course, there will be times when board members and superintendents differ. So, when they are in accord on big issues, they must demonstrate the reasoning for that unity in their messages.

Siblings don't always play well together. Some coworkers shouldn't be paired on a project. Partisan politicians are going to disagree—sometimes publicly, and often loudly. So, there should be no surprise in occasional discord between superintendents and school board members, or among the members themselves. But tolerance of education leaders' conflicts often wanes when *occasional* becomes *frequent* or, worse, *regular* disagreement.

    In the worst-case scenario, stakeholders' confidence can dissipate—not just in the leaders themselves but also in the validity of the leaders' decisions. Boards of education and their superintendents often are viewed only within the scope of their different leadership roles. In reality, these leaders form a core team essential in school districts everywhere. In many cases, the foundation for these teams' effectiveness, or the lack thereof, is set by the overall communication strategies they choose to employ.

The famous leadership coach Zig Ziglar said, "In many ways, effective communication begins with mutual respect, communication that inspires, encourages others to do their best." High-performing districts have high-performing boards of education that effectively communicate their visions, strategic goals, and information pertinent to the general public. Frequently, school boards rely on the superintendent to help convey its collective message.

The key phrase here is "collective message" for the board of education and superintendent. Sometimes, that's easier said than done. (In chapter 3, we will address handling those situations—that we all hope will be infrequent—in which real differences of opinion will be communicated.) As humans, it's natural that each board member and superintendent will tend to communicate from her or his specific viewpoint. However, whenever possible, it's vital that the board and the superintendent communicate as a team.

Though personal ideas, values, and agendas will always be present, the need for a unified message cannot be underestimated. We contend that a unified message does not silence the individual board member—as every member of the board must have a voice in developing a shared and collaborative message. The board chair and superintendent are responsible for ensuring that every member of the board is active in developing the team's message to reduce the possibility of public disagreements.

The word "we" cannot be overemphasized in the relationship between the board of education and superintendent. Board and superintendent relationships can be complex. They have different, sometimes competing, roles, but they need each other to provide effective leadership for the district. To be clear, board members are elected or appointed; superintendents are hired or elected, hopefully with the desire to do something positive for students. Creating positive outcomes for students must be the "North Star" that forms the uniting relationship between boards of education and the superintendent. From the desire to create positive outcomes for students, a unified message should form in all matters.

No one member of the board or the superintendent can do anything in isolation. Better yet, they shouldn't want to do anything in isolation. Collaboration always results in active engagement and empowerment. Through collaboration, each board member and the superintendent can still be part of developing a message, ensuring their views are conveyed while still sending a unified message.

The public—constituents, parents, faculty, and staff members—pays attention to what is said by board members and superintendents. If there are competing messages, the public can begin to question the effectiveness of districts and their leaders. Additionally, competing messages foment competing factions within the district, instead of everyone working toward the same goal of helping every student earn a quality education that prepares them for college or a career.

The public is quick to recognize dissensions between the school board and the superintendent. Nothing conveys "trouble on the horizon" more than different messages between a school board and the superintendent. There is no "I" when it comes to boards of education and superintendents, just like in any other leadership roles. Members of the board of education and the superintendent should be cautioned from using the word "I," even subtly.

The word "we" should be heard and clearly conveyed repeatedly in board meetings, in press releases, and in public face-to-face meetings. No matter how successful the outcome or size of the failure, "we" should resonate throughout the message. With "we," there is no pointing fingers but, instead, a collaborative reflection of how the team—the board of education and superintendent—could do things differently that will result in a success.

PRACTICAL STRATEGIES

- *Develop a strategic vision and communicate this vision regularly and consistently.* When the board communicates about any topic, issue, or policy, the message should always relate to the strategic vision for the district. When the board communicates the vision, there is no place for a singular voice but, instead, a united voice.
- *Ensure the board has clear roles for communication.* In many cases, the board chair should be the face of communication for the board. Together, the chair and superintendent can communicate agreement in decision making. Whenever possible, individual board members should work closely with the board chair or vice chair, the superintendent, the public relations officer, or all these individuals to make sure that the message is in line with the overall goals of the board.
- *Understand the superintendent works for the board in most cases and communicates the board's message.* Superintendents should not be communicating their personal views alone but, instead, the views of the board team. The superintendent can only communicate the message of the board if the superintendent and board have strong, positive, and collegial working relationships based on trust. Too often, those relationships can derail because of a loss of trust, a breach of confidentiality, or a failure to communicate the leadership team's message accurately.
- *View communication as a tool that helps bring the district's and board's vision to fruition.* Effective communication requires practice and a team that possesses a variety of exceptional communication skills. The board, even if

it is not required, should receive annual communication training; likewise, the superintendent should also engage in ongoing communication training. Communication must be diverse using a variety of tools—e-mail, press releases, social media, the district's website, face-to-face meetings, video conferences, and such. To be on top and to be considered exceptional at communication, boards and superintendents must be engaged in training specifically focused on how to communicate as a team, not a team of individuals.
- *Be transparent.* Though we mentioned this earlier briefly, the board and superintendent must have an open relationship—where each member of the board and superintendent are able to share information and are not afraid to ask questions. The superintendent needs supportive board members. Likewise, board members need a superintendent who is their source of accurate information to share with the general public.
- *Recognize the importance of each board member and their concerns, expertise, and goals.* Boards need to communicate one message; however, each board member must feel as if they have had a voice in developing the message. This is where the superintendent's role becomes important: he or she must help ensure that every voice is heard, valued, and conveyed in developing an overall message for the board. Though there will be times when board members have different views, consensus and compromise is essential to effective and high-performing boards of education. Furthermore, compromise is important to developing a unified message. If board members have a great working relationship among themselves and with the superintendent, even dissenting board members can support the message—or may be able to live with a message of consensus—as their voices were valued.

KEY TAKEAWAY

It's "we" before "I" when it comes to the board of education and superintendent. The board of education and the superintendent must be a team if the district expects to move forward. Both the board of education and the superintendent must recognize and support the belief that they serve to better the outcomes for every student, not to advance personal ideologies, values, or beliefs, or for personal gain.

This is not to say that personal views should be silenced. What must be emphasized is consensus building; team members must work across personal agendas to form a collaborative and unified message that students are more important than any individual. Boards of education and superintendents must take the time to work together, put differences aside, and realize that collaboration and teamwork makes the dream work.

Chapter Three

Communicating When Leaders Differ

**Board of Education
Superintendent**

> *Educator and author Peter Drucker said, "Only three things happen naturally in organizations: friction, confusion, and underperformance. Everything else requires leadership." These complexities can be found in school districts and in the team dynamics of boards of education.*

Parents know young siblings don't always play well together. Supervisors know some coworkers just shouldn't be paired on a project. And, perhaps frustratingly, voters have come to know that state and federal lawmakers on different sides of the political aisle are going to disagree, sometimes publicly, often loudly.

So, it should come as no surprise when there is occasional discord between superintendents and school board members, or among the members themselves. But public tolerance of education leaders' conflicts often begins to wane when *occasional* becomes *frequent* or, even worse, *regular* disagreement. In the worst-case scenario, stakeholders' confidence can dissipate—not just in the leaders themselves but also in the validity of the leaders' decisions about managing district operations and supporting student achievement.

What those stakeholders need to see—and hear—is evidence that even short-term conflicts don't demonstrate an inability to work together for the greater good of children. In most cases, boards of education are political boards; therefore, politics is almost certain to enter the discussion. With that said, superintendents and boards of education must work together to find common ground where progress continues in the district. There is no room or time for boards of education and superintendents to become entangled in meaningless spats or disagreements. It's perfectly fine to disagree with each other, but not to the point that the work of leading and governing is compromised.

THE BOARD/SUPERINTENDENT TEAM VOICE

Negatives naturally attract attention, so school leaders are advised to underscore the working, collaborative team with public evidence. When the administration has produced exceptional research, completed a beneficial initiative, or created an innovative solution to a problem, that's worth recognition by the board members.

When the board makes a tough vote—one that supports the administration but disappoints some stakeholders—the superintendent can take note of the difficulty of the decision, the consideration of constituents' input, and especially any modifications in the final action plan that resulted directly from board member questions or suggestions.

Sometimes, but not always, meeting audience members will hear and remember such comments. At the very least, supportive statements can fortify the image of a unified board team. But let's face it. Board members and superintendents are people, too, and we all tend to remember when the fruits of our work are appreciated.

Understand this: In no way are these recommendations to be taken as advocating an agreement-over-all-else approach to district leadership. For example, sometimes decisions that benefit one school or one part of a district will carry a potentially negative effect elsewhere. It should be hard—maybe unfair—to expect the board member with an adverse impact on her or his division to be an enthusiastic supporter of such plans in all cases.

At the same time, superintendents make difficult recommendations that frequently net a unanimous board vote of agreement. Board members should consider offering more than their "Yes" votes to the conversation. On the controversial issues, constituents deserve to know why their representatives favored the administration's plan. It shouldn't be a defensive response. Nor does it need to be fawning support of the superintendent or a strident rejection of opposing viewpoints. A reasoned, explanatory statement of the factors that led to the decision is another tool in the board member's communications toolkit.

A VOTE . . . BUT ALSO A VOICE

And that leads to a vital communications consideration that every school board member should ponder. Every month of every year, thousands of local school board members across the United States perform a shared duty—they vote. They vote on budgets and bond issues, policies and personnel, calendars and contracts, and closing and opening buildings, and the list—if not endless—certain is more extensive than needs to be addressed here.

Board members also take their oaths of office with a function of service that arguably can be just as powerful as their votes, and that is the public use of their voices. Too often, the voices of school board members are woefully underused, a lost asset in the ongoing quest to raise public understanding—and support—of public education.

The board member voice most frequently gets exercised at the board meeting. But even there, it can be underused. If the board is divided, who usually gets quoted in the newspaper story? Those would be the "No" votes from the minority side. Why is that? Mostly it is because folks who come out on the short side of things tend to make their case, while officials who came out ahead just want to take the "win" and get out of there.

But how does the public gauge the decisions of the majority when no one offers reasons for their votes? Even when the board is united, actions of major importance merit some explanation to constituents. Some may agree, and others may disagree; but the board members who speak up have exercised the crucial second half of their voting role—by using their voice.

While board members on the minority side of an action have a right to express themselves, it's crucial that it begins and ends with that meeting. Repeated reminders of one's objections to a decided issue aid no one and certainly not the board team. Nor do they help the dissenting member in the long run; rather, that voice can become relegated to being seen as a dissenter just for the sake of dissenting.

That perception can diminish a member's impact and influence in future debates and decisions. Remember: the colleague you have disagreed with on a past board vote will be a potential partner on a divisive matter in the future. The impact of board member voice isn't limited to board meetings. Individual expressions (which should also be noted in all uses as speaking for oneself) can reach stakeholders through social media posts, letters to the editor, e-mails to constituents, participation in public forums, and the most routine venue—one-to-one conversations.

As elected (and in some cases, appointed) representatives, the most effective board members are the ones who listen the most. And the board members who have the greatest impact frequently are those who—having taken the time to listen and learn—then use whatever communications opportunities they favor to share that knowledge with stakeholders and especially their board constituents.

Statutes require board member votes. There are no such mandates for use of the board members' voices. How often or rarely board members avail themselves of this option is a personal choice. But consider this: a board member who opts not to make maximum use of his or her official voice also removes a valuable communication resource from the whole board, for the achievement of its students and as part of the overall advocacy for a strong public education system.

PRACTICAL STRATEGIES

- *Find common ground.* This is where the superintendent plays a huge role. The superintendent, in most cases, must be the middleman between board members. During controversial votes or votes that may split the board, the superintendent will need to help the board arrive at a vote. Hot topic issues and controversial votes may require the superintendent to "work" the board, finding common ground so that disagreements are not on display during meetings or do not spill out into the public. Forming consensus is still OK, even as the art of compromise is challenged or may not be acceptable.
- *Be open.* One of the worst things that can happen is that both the superintendent and individual board members decide to go to their respective corners and refuse to speak. Superintendents and board members must embrace their roles as leaders and governors (so to speak) with an open mind—open to new ideas and new ways of doing things. When superintendents and boards of education become a team at the time of hiring the superintendent, there needs to be clear expectations and processes when differences appear as, assuredly, they will appear from time to time. Working through differences is paramount to the overall success of the district and, more important, to the students.
- *Understand the importance of the office.* More often than one would think, superintendents and members of the board yearn for the title of the office but not the responsibilities that come with the associated role. Working past differences is incumbent of the role of the superintendent and each

board member. Taking on the associated role and responsibilities of each critical position in the district requires far more than casting a dissenting vote or failure to work in a team-like fashion. Personal goals, motives, and aspirations must be put aside in order to move the district forward. The role of the superintendent and board members requires dedication, focus, and an unwavering understanding not to get caught up in petty disagreements or sleek winds of change from unsubstantiated theories.

KEY TAKEAWAY

Differences will almost certainly occur. The key is to make sure that differences do not derail the work of the board and the superintendent as a team. Keep critical differences private. Voice concerns about votes publicly when necessary; however, keep the work professional, and work behind the scenes to overcome key differences. Teachers, staff, parents, and the community are almost certain to view public disagreements as signs of dysfunction. Dysfunction among the superintendent and board of education members is not good for the team nor for the district, the faculty, staff, or students.

Chapter Four

Board Meetings and Messages

Regular, planned communications about board meetings can go a long way toward keeping the public engaged and creating pathways for understanding when tough decisions arise.

School board meetings feature discussions—sometimes debates and always decision making. But they're also opportunities—before, during, and after—as key communications tools for board members and superintendents. Many board meeting communications appropriately are handled by the district administration.

Many superintendents view the biweekly or monthly board meeting as the conduit to refocusing everyone on the essential work of the district—student success. High-performing school districts ensure that board meetings are about the essential work and not noise. But there is a balance. Too much educational jargon can turn off stakeholders but, more important, disengage board members, as many are not educators. Superintendents and other school administrators must work to educate board members and the general public through the board meeting.

Many board meeting communications appropriately are handled by the district administration. Advance notices to the media and the public are almost universally required by state law. But let's face it. Sometimes, school board governance is routine, not at all newsworthy, and not every board meeting presents a full array of communications opportunities for board leaders. The key is no matter what is on the board docket, the meetings are transparent and publicized according to local policies and state rules.

And yet meeting agendas don't have to have blockbuster action items to merit public attention or be effective. Members of the board of education and superintendent must recognize that even the smallest agenda item can garner public support or push back. Though some agenda items are constant, team members must study and understand each agenda item and weigh the positives and negatives of each one—the more prepared for the board meeting everyone is, the more productive the meeting will become. To be clear, all board meetings are important.

Furthermore, members of the board and the superintendent must work together prior to the meeting so that there are no surprises. Everyone should be on the same page so that the work of the board remains focused on what matters the most—the success of students and the district. Transparency with the general public is not the only requirement for a high-functioning board. Transparency between each board member and the superintendent, sharing of information, and keeping surprises out of board meetings are vision critical.

BEFORE THE MEETING

There is virtually always some topic and/or action at every school board meeting that local leaders wish was understood by their communities. But there are ways to increase the chances of that happening. One way is for superintendents to draw attention to specific items on the agenda when the notice is sent to local media outlets. It can be as simple as highlighting the item or attaching a note with a couple of paragraphs of background information. Remember that if your local media typically covers your board meetings, reporters will find *something* to write about, so why not pitch a story idea with the agenda?

When a topic up for board action is particularly complex or wide ranging in its impact, an advance briefing for local reporters is a solid option. It's good to spell out your facts so reporters clearly grasp your reasoning for proposals and/or actions by the board. Board members who are active on social media can alert followers/friends of agenda items, even encouraging meeting attendance. But be wary of doing so primarily in order to boost attendance of supporters for your side in a debatable decision.

More and more school districts are also using social media to release board meeting notices and to bring attention to particular topics of interest. Districts are embracing and becoming more effective with the use of social media, after years of some trepidation. Social media is creating a new level of transparency between boards of education and the general public. If done correctly, there is an increasing opportunity to bridge informational gaps that may have existed in the past.

DURING THE MEETING

- *Student presentations.* School board meetings should be a showcase of school success stories. It would be hard—if not impossible—to argue that there aren't enough positive things happening for even the smallest school system to have a "good news agenda item" for each meeting. And it need not lengthen the meeting nor cause a planning nightmare for the staff. Student presentations almost always send encouraging messages, and a student-led demonstration of academic learning can be even more powerful than the most data-driven staff report on the same subject (or, even better, done in tandem).

    Just a scratch-the-surface sample of ideas could include student science fair exhibits, quick recall or future problem-solving challenges, literacy skills building and engineering design projects, and much more. As many board members will attest, they prefer to hear from students more than any other district stakeholder. Likewise, board members appreciate when students are recognized, mentioned, and celebrated in their board meetings. Also, board meetings should always start and end on a positive note, and student achievement or recognitions always seem to unite boards—as board members, at the end of the day, are there to help advance student success through their governance.
- *Public comment periods.* How the public participates in board meetings is almost exclusively a decision for the board members. Some—but not all—states' open meetings laws require public comment periods. The best guidance for representative government engagement at such functions is

to have a set of rules, and then follow them. Produce a handout that spells out how public comment will be accepted. Some boards limit individual speakers' time, while others have an overall time allowed for comments. To allow input on pending action items, it's best to have the public comment period early on in the agenda.

The board chairperson carries the heavy load of ensuring that participants in public comment periods—if you have them—are treated fairly. Restrictions against using student names and criticism of school personnel by name should be spelled out in the meeting flyer, and then followed by the chair. While there can be valid arguments on limiting public comments at board meetings, an equally persuasive case can be made for board meetings that are as inclusive to visitors as possible.

Public education today needs more engagement from the general public, rather than disengagement. A recent Gallup poll (2018) showed that 55 percent of the public surveyed were dissatisfied with public education in the United States. With this level of dissatisfaction, district administrators, boards of education, and educators must look to engage the public more, and this process begins by listening. Biweekly or monthly board meetings are public meetings, almost always in a public building, and always with public business being conducted. Accommodations so all can clearly hear the proceedings is a good place to start. Then, reasonable rules—and restrictions—on participation can be developed, usually in concert with the board attorney to ensure compliance with statutory requirements.

- *Board members' explanations of votes.* When public understanding of a particular board decision is vital, board members have a choice to make about explaining their votes in the public forum of the meeting. Even in cases where the board is unanimous in backing the superintendent's recommendation, a "yea" vote explained can have a big impact on the public's grasp of that decision. Verbal confirmation is a powerful symbol of democracy.

Of course, not all board member comments will make the media reports or even will be remembered by meeting attendees. But when an issue is of keen interest to constituents, board members have an obligation to become educators about their reasonings, pro or con. Board members must recognize that their votes matter; their votes send a strong message about the priorities of the board and each individual member. Their voting behavior also provides a compass for the day-to-day operations of the district.

One vote can create a positive lasting impact on the success of students and the district. Likewise, one vote can create a negative impact that can ultimately derail a district. Votes matter even when there are no members of the public present in the crowd. No matter how well attended the board meeting is, no matter if the press is present, how each member votes cir-

culates throughout the district and community. Board members are or will be known by the votes they cast. Though board members are political, just because they are elected, their focus must be on student success—not political agendas.
- *Transparency.* The biweekly or monthly board meeting is all about transparency. Superintendents and members of the board of education must work together to ensure that information, policies, discussions, and votes are as transparent as possible—following the laws of their state. Some things will never be discussed in a public meeting, while others should always be discussed and voted on in a public meeting.

  The effectiveness of the district and the board of education is impacted by the level of transparency that exists. Being open about decisions and involving others in the decision making through surveys, interviews, or public comment helps the district administration and the board of education establish a culture of transparency, which will lead to positive support from the public.
- *Following the meeting.* Finally, consider what is to be done to communicate about the board's decisions following the meeting. There may be mainstream media coverage. The "watercooler method" of spreading the word may work sometimes. But in this era of social media messaging, there can be multiple versions of what took place being spread before you even get into your vehicle to head home from the meeting. Some of these examples will be accurate depictions of what the board did; sadly, others will be misrepresentations—some innocent and some not so. Superintendents and school boards are well advised not to leave the education of their communities about their decisions all in the hands of others. There are plenty of options to reach the targeted audience: a post-session summary on the district website or social media platforms, a news release, or an e-mail blast to employees and stakeholders. These can be regular post-meeting communications tools or be limited situations when it's imperative that the board's message gets out in a factual, timely instrument.

To be clear, no board or district needs to use all of these communications opportunities after every meeting. But school board meetings afford leaders so much more than just time each month to conduct the district's business. Board meetings can be a unique and important communications instrument to increase public perceptions about—and potentially support for—district leaders' decision making.

PRACTICAL STRATEGIES

- *Make meetings as transparent as possible.* Community attendance at board meetings is always based on the community and always what is on the agenda. A good rule of thumb is to publicize board meeting agendas online, via social media, and in local newspapers as much as possible. Let the community stakeholders know what the board will be discussing and approving. The more transparent and open the meetings are, the better the board of education and superintendent will be viewed by the public.
- *Make the meetings strategic.* Don't forget the purpose of board meetings. Board meetings help drive the work of the district each day. The board establishes the mission, vision, and core beliefs in the district. Therefore, the board meeting should be focused on the mission, vision, and core beliefs. An effective and good strategy is to align each agenda item to strategic processes in the district. A strategic alignment also encourages boards to develop strategic plans for the district. To be a high-performing school district and board of education, there is no room for shooting from the hip. There must be a clear need for the agenda item.
- *Communicate meetings in multiple ways.* Nothing says transparent or open like broadcasting the monthly board meeting, sharing meeting agendas in multiple formats, or live tweeting during the board meeting. Many boards of education are now broadcasting their meetings online or via social media. Now constituents can access the board meetings from anywhere and see precisely what the board discusses each month, which is typically a gold star for high-performing school boards and school districts. Furthermore, many boards of education and school districts are now live tweeting items in queue and board actions in real time. This not only provides followers updated information but also provides an unofficial record of board minutes.

KEY TAKEAWAY

We cannot emphasize enough the necessity and importance of transparency in the communication process of the board of education and the superintendent. Just as the superintendent and board of education need to be in regular communication with each other, both need to be communicating with constituents regarding board meetings—no matter if it is a monthly, biweekly, or special meeting. The more the board and the superintendent keep constituents up to date with meetings and agenda items, the more constituents will be supportive of decisions. The belief that constituents will support decisions when decisions are transparent is true when it comes to the board of education and superintendent.

Chapter Five

Taking Families from Informed to Engaged

Sadly, the value and potential impact of a planned, regular course of internal communications is too often an overlooked resource by organizations, including schools—and their school boards. Effective leaders should consider the effort essential, not optional.

A group taking a tour at a huge automobile manufacturing plant found itself in a lengthy holding pattern. As the group's guide chatted with her guests, she called over a member of the plant's custodial team who was working nearby to join in the discussion. For a couple of minutes, the janitor told his audience not about his personal work but, rather, about how the "team" was producing one of America's best-selling, safest, most highly rated family automobiles. And he didn't just speak in generalities. He mentioned some of the features of this vehicle that set it apart from competitors' cars.

A planned performance? Perhaps. There were engineers and production workers available. The company fostered a reputation for its team approach to the workplace. The desired message was clear: this was a quality-centered environment where employees who might never install a brake or check out a seat belt felt they contributed to the end result—a vehicle that gave them pride on the assembly line, in the dealership showroom, and, most important, on the roadways.

But that took more than individual pride; it required a sharing of information . . . information about their work, about goals, and about results. How many school board members or superintendents would bring a group of citizens to visit a middle school and expect the cafeteria worker, the classroom aide, or the attendance clerk to elaborate about what takes place in the building's classrooms? Here's a more pertinent question: What can superintendents and boards of education do to foster school environments where every employee is empowered with knowledge and encouraged to be willing to help tell the story of her/his school?

One key component is the regularity and effort made to keep the school "family" in the loop. And that takes leadership commitment to an effective internal communications process. The vast majority of school boards and superintendents work in school districts that struggle with internal communications. Employees, school board members, and even superintendents are often voicing concern about the lack of cohesive messages, accurate information, and leaked internal communications about information not yet ready for the public.

IT STARTS AT THE TOP

When school boards conduct annual evaluations of superintendents, one almost universal metric that gets gauged is that of communication. And often it's more than the superintendent's involvement in news media interviews, presentations to civic groups, or congratulatory letters to students and staff. An effective superintendent must be known in the district's top leadership circle for a steady flow of pertinent information.

Successful superintendents are those who ensure that all board members know of major happenings—good, bad, and developing—within their district. No school board member should read about a problem on the front page of the local newspaper or hear it as the lead story on the midday newscast without having received a heads up from the superintendent. This doesn't mean that the superintendent will be able to answer all board members' questions immediately. It simply means—as one veteran school leader training expert offered in seminars for years—no surprises or, at the very least, the earnest effort to limit those surprises that can't be avoided.

Time and time again, the relationship between the board of education and superintendent fall apart not because of personality, policy, or direction of the district issues but, instead, because of the level of communication. Taking seconds to send board members an e-mail or text with details of a situation or news story is a major relationship builder. Believe it or not, the relationship between the board of education and the superintendent must be based on transparency, respect, and communication. The board needs a superintendent who is transparent with them and who can communicate with them during the good and bad times. The superintendent needs a board who is willing to listen and help him or her convey correct information and who is willing to be patient as details of situations or issues are gathered—which rarely happens in 5 minutes.

This "no surprises" approach truly represents a two-way street for district leaders. Board members—at least those not working to put themselves in the spotlight—will alert the superintendent before taking a public position of opposition to an administration recommendation. Building and maintaining trust among leaders is an ongoing challenge. District leaders often face working relationships sufficiently tough enough without always having to watch one's backside for an unexpected confrontation. Leaders will disagree from time to time (as we will explore in greater detail in a later chapter). The emphasis must be on open, frequent exchanges of ideas among those atop the district leadership organizational chart.

AFTER ACTING, BEGIN SHARING

Social media has overtaken the watercooler as the workplace source of mixing rumor and fact. So, school leaders are tasked with finding the best ways to inform district staff when decisions of significance have been made. To be clear, details shouldn't be sacrificed for speed; leaders can combat inaccurate speculation with the facts presented in a timely manner. Practicing patience can help prevent larger issues for all those involved, including board members and the superintendent. For board members and superintendents in the age of quick information, the need for *quick* information must never be the practice because there is always too much at stake. *Accurate* information must be the desire—as soon as possible.

A regular board action report to all school personnel can be a real asset. The key is regularity—something those wanting facts and additional information can expect following each meeting. This can be the night of the board meeting, the following morning, or even several days later. Again, the standard is creating among the school workforce the idea that explanations of action will be forthcoming. Again, we cannot stress transparency enough. Providing board members and school workforce limited details is always a red flag; more is more, not less is more, with board members, workforce, and superintendent communications.

Such a regular board action report also can be a boon to board members who make extra efforts to keep others informed. Some board members have constituent e-mail lists; others have web blogs. The action report can be an easy resource that also improves the odds of a common message being delivered across the community.

Finally, this post-action report can generate positive press coverage. Reporters are always in need of ideas for tomorrow's story. In many communities, shrinking newsrooms mean less coverage of board meetings—other than for a controversy or confrontation—and the post-meeting report details about a recognition, a redirection of resources, or an issue that leaders are working to resolve can become the start of a news article that enlightens multiple target audiences of the board/superintendent team.

ENCOURAGING ATMOSPHERES OF SHARING

How each superintendent chooses to get information out to district personnel is going to depend on the "communications comfort level" of the individual leader. Some are fine with all-staff e-mails, while others may craft and post a memo on an employees-only web page. Unit-by-unit and school-by-school meetings may take place for big ticket issues of broad interest. When that's not possible, a video commentary by the chief executive officer can add a personal element to the same facts laid out in black and white.

While the delivery tool can vary, what should be consistent is the leader's encouragement that facts, figures, and objective analysis be shared with school personnel at all levels. Think about it this way: each superintendent, each division manager, and each building principal has her or his own personal circle of influence, and the other people in those circles can be educational assets if they are given essential information. And don't forget about the circles of influence among teachers, clerks, custodians, bus drivers, and aides. Those employees have friends who are parents and taxpayers, and they all have opinions and voices.

Highly effective district leaders know what information they can and should share. The next step is to foster an environment where everyone from mid-level managers to building-level staff value both the quality of job- and/or district-related information and then see themselves as key communicators of that information to those in their personal circles. Likewise, a culture where accurate, transparent, and cross-sectional information is the expectation is precisely how school districts, boards of education, and superintendents become high performing.

PRACTICAL STRATEGIES

- *Old school—the employee bulletin board*: Yes, they still exist, and for some employees, they remain a regular source of information. Any all-staff e-mail has just as much of a place printed and posted in the bus garage and in the teachers' lounge as it does in everyone's inbox.
- *New school—more effective e-mails*: The importance of the subject line for e-mails is like the headline of a newspaper story—you've got to grab the readers' attention and be totally honest with the subsequent content. Too many subject lines of IMPORTANT or READ NOW diminish the impact, and it's hard to tell just how many e-mails with those subject lines get sent before the recipient reaches for the delete button. Take a moment to acknowledge the routine and then to genuinely reflect the more essential missives.
- *Sharing socially*: Don't be shy about asking that an important post on your Facebook or Twitter platforms be retweeted or shared. Remember those varied circles of influence. Admittedly, there are too many negatives about how some people use social media. But don't underestimate the extra impact of retransmitted facts to those who value someone enough to like or friend a person's social media page. But you may have to actually ask for the retweet or the share to maximize the potential.

KEY TAKEAWAY

Every school operates within a district that exists within a community of the engaged and the unengaged. Efforts to build an informed employee base—and an inclination to be part of the school/district information pipeline to the greater public—can achieve two important purposes: broadened understanding of education-related issues and nurtured confidence in those superintendents and board of education members who have been charged with finding solutions in the interest of the student in the classroom.

Chapter Six

Two-Way Communicating via the News Media

Board of Education

Superintendent

Even as newsrooms and audiences shrink, public opinion on education is affected by mainstream media coverage. Effective reporter interactions remain on school leaders' to-do list.

With just under 100,000 American public schools in operation, it's a safe bet that every day thousands of school leaders respond to a call, text, e-mail, or face-to-face inquiry from a reporter. The contact can range from controversial to highly positive, complex to simple, a single-story question to an ongoing issue. No interview or information request should be taken lightly, even with a reporter whom you know. But when superintendents and board members ask, "What if I get a media call about this?," they create the opportunity to be prepared to address the situation.

Yes, working with reporters can be stressful. No interview or information request should be taken lightly, even with a reporter with whom you've had prior involvement. But when superintendents and board members ask themselves, "What if I get a media call?," they almost always are better prepared to handle an aspect of leadership that "comes with the territory." Board members and superintendents are public servants; therefore, they must be ready to serve publicly—even if the service is performed by communicating with the general public through the medium of newspapers, radio, or television.

Unquestionably, the vast majority of press inquiries go to the school and district administration. But school board members should never assume that working with the media is a job for the superintendent. When the board takes action, it is the board—and often its individual members—who are called upon to explain. In such cases, the board's "voice" is the most appropriate and effective approach to reaching the public through the news media. (We'll discuss more on the board "voice" in a later chapter.)

And, as we will explore in this chapter, media relations truly must be a two-way information street. You have a right to promote story ideas, to question unfair or incomplete coverage, and to engage mainstream news media to tell your district's story to readers, listeners, and viewers who are your employees, parents, and taxpayers.

WHEN A REPORTER CALLS

Some simple best practices go a long way to creating the best options when involved in media contacts, even when the ultimate story won't be as pleasant as you'd like.

- When you get a reporter's inquiry, ask questions before you start providing answers. Get a clear picture of what the story is about, especially if there are aspects that may be debated by people on differing sides.
- If you determine the appropriate person to respond is someone like the superintendent, the board chair, or a department head, explain and refer the reporter to the alternative source (and then *immediately* alert that person to expect the call and what you've learned about the story).
- Board members should avoid attempting to or appearing to attempt to speak for the administration. By the same logic, the administration should not say to a reporter, "The board did this because . . ." Keeping those separate lines of communications, responsibility can reduce the incidents of confusion about recommendations' and decision making.
- If you need to get more information, or just need to think a bit before answering a reporter's question, ask what the deadline is for the story, assure the journalist a response well ahead of that time, and make certain that happens.

- Plan what you want to say by developing a short set of talking points. For example, take a post-meeting inquiry about a vote on school taxes. Point #1 may be the primary reason why a member voted a certain way. Point #2 may be the human factors (raising student achievement, tax costs to fixed-income families, impact on parents of a schedule change) weighed by the board member in reaching a conclusion. And point #3 may state what benefits the board member feels will be achieved going forward from the decision, or how the member is open to additional input on a pending decision.
- If you determine there is confusion on the reporter's part due to misunderstanding of an issue or possibly misinformation given by someone purposely misleading the reporter, acknowledge the other view—but make your case as to the validity of what you are saying. A superintendent who concedes that there are other points of view while staking out a position speaks from a stronger position than simply saying the other guy/gal is wrong. And you can give the reporter pause about how or even whether to use that other source's information.
- Avoid saying "no comment." The story will be printed, broadcast, or posted online, and your side won't be reflected. There is always something you can say. For example: An employee has been accused of a criminal act involving a student. You have policies in place for dealing with such investigations and training of employees to prevent such incidents, and you can talk about these in general without discussing a specific case. Just don't say, "I can't talk about that." Rather, explain limitations such as things like education right to privacy laws or personnel policies.
- Never lie to a reporter. If you don't know, say so, but don't offer something in responding to a reporter that you aren't certain is factual.

INITIATING A CALL TO A REPORTER

There are all sorts of reasons for school leaders to take the initiative in contacting the media: pitching story ideas, taking note of inaccuracies in stories, promoting upcoming events of public interest, or seeking clarification of a point in a story that may have caused confusion. Even in situations where there is an ongoing disagreement over coverage, tomorrow's newspaper or today's midday radio or TV reporter is going to be read/seen/heard by a mixed audience—some will know only of the subject matter of today's news.

Clearly, school leaders who reach out to reporters need to understand that there are a limited number of inches of copy in each newspaper edition, as well as a limited number of seconds in every newscast. And you don't get to decide which story is more or less worthy for inclusion in the report. But if no one makes the pitch, or draws attention to an error, the opportunity for greater public clarity is lost for sure.

Here are some ideas that work when you begin a conversation with a reporter:

- The broader the appeal of the story—and thus sometimes the less of the focus on you as a school leader—the greater the potential for interest to provide coverage. There is a difference in a story about a superintendent capturing a grant for the district compared to how those funds are going to be used to educate children. A board member's long-standing advocacy that is realized in a new school program may only be part of a more viable story about how that program benefits children and their community. Remember IAK: It's about kids.
- Make a leader-initiative contact as personal as you feel comfortable doing. This can be as simple as forwarding an announcement e-mail. Or you can add your own insights into an issue along with your thoughts on how the public might benefit from knowing about how the district is responding to an issue. (Be aware that you are "on the record" in doing so and what you include in the e-mail might wind up in a story quote. That's fine, too; just be selective in what you say.)
- On the subject of "off the record," it's always best to assume that you are always "on the record" when talking with a reporter. Some communications practitioners successfully use the "off the record" tool to further clarify about a complex or sensitive matter. That approach probably only works when you are working with a reporter you know and trust. Regardless of what you may have seen in a movie, trying to go back later and claim "now that was 'off the record' and you can't use it" is usually a nonstarter with a good reporter.
- If you have a problem with a printed/broadcast story, take a moment and do a little analysis. Were you really misquoted or quoted out of context, or can you see how there might be an honest misunderstanding? Is a minor (by your measure) error in a story worth drawing attention to? (Any error of significance merits a conversation with the reporter. Sometimes you may ask for a correction; often, you may simply be bringing correct information or at least a different point of view to the reporter's awareness. The point is that not every error any of us make is worth a complaint.)
- Take issues of coverage up first with the reporter rather than going to a news director or publisher with the initial concern. If there is no satisfaction, then move up the chain of command. Make your ultimate goal the most accurate coverage going forward rather than gaining acknowledgment of problems

with earlier stories. Superintendents have turned local media coverage of their districts around 180 degrees through such conversations. It's not a guarantee, but it's almost always worth the time and the talk.
- In working with newspapers, the letter to the editor column can still be a useful tool, and not just to take issue with media coverage. Your approach may be to offer that different point of view or to expand on a point that you believe didn't get its full exploration in the story. As letters to the editor are usually word-count limited, your letters should be more about making your point and less about attacking the story or critics who were quoted therein.
- If you appreciate a story, it's perfectly appropriate to let a reporter know.
- Keep pitching ideas because perseverance gets rewarded, even if not as often as you'd like.

There always will be a degree of "adversarial relationship" between reporters and public officials. That's what is supposed to keep everyone in the equation honest with each other. There are going to be agenda-driving news deciders, and there are going to be school leaders who make questionable decisions. The best relationships arise from when media and source work to avoid any degree of long-term animosity.

School leaders who choose to ignore local media when it doesn't suit them are unlikely to suddenly gain an impartial ear in times of controversy. In today's "round-the-clock news cycle," fueled by instant reporting via social media, an earnest working relationship between journalists and school leaders almost always proves beneficial in terms of more accurate reporting and greater public understanding of school goals, challenges, opportunities, and actions.

PRACTICAL STRATEGIES

- *Align your district's media relations strategy to the district's vision or mission.* Just as the district's vision or mission drives the teaching and learning process, so should the vision and mission drive the school's media relations strategy. Connect the district's vision and mission to the following questions:

    1. Why is media important to the school's mission and vision?
    2. How can the media help communicate the school district's mission and vision?

- *Understand the purpose of the media relations strategy.* The main purpose of the district's media strategy is to inform, engage, and empower all stakeholder groups in the district's journey. School superintendents and boards of education cannot, alone, provide the best quality education to students. Educating a student takes a village, and your media relations strategy is the strategic process to connect stakeholders with the overarching goals of the district to ultimately help educate students and ensure that they are college and career ready.

- *Use a variety of tools in the media strategy.* Too often, superintendents and boards of education develop a media strategy that only includes one media tool, for instance, social media. By utilizing one media tool to reach stakeholders, school districts overlook stakeholder groups. The media strategy must include radio, face-to-face interactions, town-hall meetings, newspaper, website, social media, handouts (i.e., monthly take-home newsletters), and television (if possible). A diverse media strategy can help the district inform, engage, and empower all stakeholder groups.
- *Diversify the content that is being delivered in your media strategy.* High-performing school districts deliver news, post pictures, and share information items. School superintendents and boards of education should find the right balance—which will lead to more stakeholders paying attention to the messages being released. Stakeholders need district news, pictures, informational items, and important notifications (like school closings, etc.). Relying solely on one piece of media leads to disengagement of stakeholders, which may gradually lead to loss of support of the district's vision and mission.
- *Keep the media strategy simple.* No one likes the person or organization who sends 25 e-mails a day. Moderation is key to keeping stakeholders engaged and listening to the news, celebrations, recognitions, information, and updates that the district shares via social media, in newspapers, or online. Think about times of the day when the messages will get the highest number of views or when e-mails will most likely be read.
- *Form partnerships with local news agencies and reporters.* The district's message needs to get out using all outlets, including the radio, newspaper, and news station. Reporters can be your best friend when it comes to the district's messaging and also getting important information and notification out to the general public. Take time to form these vision-critical partnerships with local reporters.

KEY TAKEAWAY

School superintendents and school boards must recognize the importance of a media relations strategy. A media relations strategy is just as important as having a strategy to raise test scores—it takes upfront considerations, patience, and a commitment to transparency (or as much as legally possible). Many school districts refer to media relations strategy as a communication guide. Some school districts will have an elaborate and detailed media strategy with a chief information officer or director of public relations leading the strategy.

But even the smallest, most rural school district needs a media strategy—to keep the message focused, simple, and always in the best interests of students. Too often, school districts fall victim to what some call "big messaging" that honestly doesn't inform, engage, or empower stakeholders but, instead, does the opposite. The message must always be simple and focused on students. Parents, guardians, community members, and business leaders want to know how the information, news, or message shared impacts student achievement.

Chapter Seven

Know When to Talk and Know When to Hold Back

Knowledge is power, and power carries responsibilities. School leaders constantly possess information that legally and ethically must be kept to themselves. But they also face choices involving matters about which the public has a right to know.

Spot quiz: You are a school board member in a district that's considering replacing an antiquated school. That much is public fact and has begun to generate inquiries on where the new facility will be located. Several parcels of land have been considered. The district is in initial negotiations with a property owner. Rumor of the talks spark critical posts on social media, and you begin getting questions from constituents.

What can you say? That's pretty simple. Nothing has been decided. Discussing a specific site during negotiations could negatively affect the final deal—both in terms of seller willingness and an ultimate taxpayer cost. Talks could reach an impasse, and discussions with owners of alternative plots of land might be necessary. The old saying "loose lips sink ships" is so true in the realm of bid deliberations.

Now throw in a wrinkle—much of the speculation has become focused on a site that is *not* under consideration. In fact, critics are getting pretty heated about issues from traffic on nearby roads and distance from the current school to growing opposition by neighbors who have a not-in-my-backyard way of thinking. Now what can you say? Can you affirm that the controversy-stirring property isn't being considered? Can you do that while contending you can't say which other sites are on the table? Can you address those concerns—such as traffic or relative location—which may equally apply to the site of primary focus for possible purchase?

And finally, throw in the ultimate human factor. The people posing these questions aren't just unfamiliar residents of your board division/zone. They are your spouse, longtime friends, coworkers/employees/supervisors, or others who have come to you in the past with other questions or who have supported your election to the board seat you hold. Premature release or talk of information can complicate not only professional roles but also personal roles in some manner.

The old saying "the devil is in the details" comes to mind as more specifics to a situation complicate the choices of a school leader with such a dilemma. In fact, superintendents and school board members face these types of what-can-I-share decisions all the time. Some can be easy outs, but many represent lose-lose propositions without careful thought before trying to give an answer.

Therefore, it's important to hire a good school board attorney who can advise the board and superintendent about each state's laws pertaining to public release of information, including what is being discussed in executive-closed sessions. Board of education members or superintendents should never just assume information can be shared. In actuality, when in doubt ask the school board attorney. Taking a few minutes out of your day to make a phone call, write an e-mail, or have a face-to-face conversation with the school board attorney can save everyone a lot of time cleaning up misinformation; in turn, the conversation could prevent damage to the board's or district's integrity and, ultimately, could prevent litigation.

NO COMMENT—THE BLACK HOLE OF COMMUNICATIONS

In the realm of communications by public officials, few phrases generate more debate and distrust than that of "no comment." In one major public opinion survey by a major PR counseling firm, more than 7 in 10 respondents who reacted to "no comment" equated that phrase with "guilty." That's not surprising considering that the average person never has been a public official in possession of information that can't (legally) or shouldn't (morally) be shared with the individual asking the question.

An argument can be made that it's easier for major corporate directors and national political figures—whose comments might devalue stocks or put lives in jeopardy—to say "no comment" compared to their school district leader counterparts. Both sets of leaders doubtless are being advised to do so by company lawyers or board attorneys working to protect their clients' interests. And that will get no argument here . . . to a point.

"No comment" also is too often a shield that can be used to avoid answering unpleasant questions. How individual superintendents and board members choose to deal with such predicaments is a matter of very personal, ethical decision making. But use of "no comment" should never be used as a disguise for anti-transparent tendencies. If "no comment" becomes the phrase of choice, constituents will begin to raise questions and also question the board's and superintendent's integrity. "Transparency," "accuracy," and "accessibility" are three terms often used with boards of education and superintendents who practice integrity.

Let's start with talking to reporters. Indeed, reporters are used to hearing "no comment" when the challenge to leaders is a tough one. It's their job to ask the question and then to reflect the response in their stories. But in certain circumstances, school leaders who consider saying "no comment" to a reporter do have important alternatives. It takes a little extra effort, but it can produce a clearer message.

There *is* a difference between simply saying "no comment" and replying, "I can't comment on that, and here is why." That's appropriately followed by an explanation of the reasons you can't give a specific reply: you can't comment because it's prohibited by law (citing the Family Educational Rights and Privacy Act [FERPA]—more on that later); it's personnel information specifically exempted from release; or there are other statutory restrictions. Don't offer this as an excuse or an apology—you are following a law that you swore an oath to adhere to or is required by the contract of your employment.

At the same time, many situations that can garner media questions for school leaders are governed by all sorts of absolutely related points that they can talk about in detail, such as regulations or board policy and procedures. In fact, boards of education and superintendents are encouraged to reference specific board policies and procedures often. Boards of education, superintendents, and school districts are only as effective as the policies and procedures created, voted on, and implemented. They can be a great tool to reference and use when it comes to when, how, and what can be communicated.

Student discipline? There are rules to be followed for the investigation and discipline of students for infractions. Threat targeting a school? There is a process for working with law enforcement to probe the threat, as well as internal consequences if the act is by a student or employee. Staff member suspended or fired for any sort of reason? Every district has a procedure for examining complaints about employees for work-related actions, plus a series of options for resolution.

Such explanations rightly may be directed to the superintendent or other chief administrators with responsibilities related to the specific incident. Board members shouldn't be afraid to tell a reporter that the superintendent is the appropriate person to respond, especially when matters that don't directly involve board-related responsibilities are at issue. The superintendent in turn then makes the call about how to handle the media inquiry.

The reality of using "no comment" with reporters is that the public sees cases of leaders under pressure who are declining to talk. That's one of the burdens of leadership. But leaders can mitigate the supposition by some that they are trying to hide something by offering an explanation, first to reporters and later if needed to constituents who raise the same questions.

We want to be crystal clear here: There absolutely are questions from reporters—and the general public as well—where it is appropriate, if not necessary, to decline to give specific information about a school matter. Our point is that "no comment" isn't a solution to every problem involving hard queries of district leaders. Alternatives exist. They require careful anticipation of the question and the options.

FERPA AND EVERYDAY CHOICES

Consider this situation that could happen in every public school across the country on a daily basis: A student enrolled in one of your schools contracts a well-known, communicable disease. The infected child was in school for some time before symptoms displayed. The youth is at home, is undergoing medical treatment, and is in serious condition. Word of the child's condition leaks out, and parents of other students want to know whether their kids are at risk.

As a school leader, you can talk until your tongue gives out about extra cleaning of the school (Question: Do you confirm the school in question or leave all schools in the district under the same scrutiny?), about consulting with medical experts, and about sharing information about early symptoms of the condition, but there will remain some parents who will pull their children from the school unless they get answers to questions including "Was my child exposed in the same class, in the lunchroom, or in the gym?" or "Who is the sick kid?" Good luck trying to explain FERPA (Family Educational Rights and Privacy Act) in that situation.

And yet, all elements noted above—the cleaning, the work with health care professionals, and each child's right to privacy—are exactly the kinds of things school leaders facing similar situations should be prepared to say and, when necessary, to repeat. No, this response won't satisfy select parents—those with reasonable concerns as well as those with irrational ultimatums. But this scenario is one of responsibility to all parents and all students. Leaders don't get to pick and choose when they identify and when they don't.

PRACTICAL STRATEGIES

- *Media relations training.* Most state superintendent associations and school board associations offer seminars on news media relations. Training that involves mock interviews and real-world situations are applicable to school leaders of any size district. Education controversies are news, and local issues can become full-blown media storms quite quickly. Tragically, incidents of violence in a school can mean almost instantaneous—and prolonged—visitations by major media outlets. A bonus of media interview training is that virtually all cases of learning how to plan responses to reporter inquiries will produce the same kinds of talking points school leaders will want to have when similar questions come from nonmedia members of the community.
- *Anticipating inquiries.* When a school-centered issue becomes a major news story at the national or statewide level, there becomes a higher possibility of local reporters deciding to do a "Could it happen here?" kind of story. Superintendents are well advised when seeing such a story to figure out what they would say if a reporter calls. A few minutes of preparation is well worth avoiding the nervous moments when the administrative assistant says that the local newspaper editor is on line 1, wanting to talk about cybersecurity in the wake of another district being hit with a ransomware attack.
- *Consistency matters.* Most leaders are more than willing to talk about positive things in the schools: a student scoring a perfect 36 on the SAT test, an educator who wins a major award, or a decision to put additional monetary support behind an instructional asset designed to boost learning. Conversely, there is more reluctance to discuss allegations of student-on-student bullying, an employee arrested for illegal activities, or cuts to one academic area when funds are being expended on a new weight room for

the football program. There is no black-and-white, decisive advice to be given here but, rather, a cautionary reminder that some people will remember leader responses from one situation to the next.
- *Calm, cool, and collected.* Board members and superintendents will be approached in schools, at church, or in the local market by one if not all of the following on a daily basis: constituents, teachers, community leaders, parents, guardians, and the news media. You will be asked about a wide range of topics, rumors, upcoming events, legislation, personnel, and even particular individual students (yes, it happens). Listen, yes, but be very careful on the information shared. If you have doubts about what you can share, take their name, number, and/or e-mail address and tell them you will get back to them but you must first check on information. This gives you time to get accurate information, consult with the board attorney, and create a response. The key is to always get back to the person. This shows that you listen, even though you may not be able to share information.

KEY TAKEAWAY

Legal prohibitions exist on the sharing of school information in many circumstances, giving leaders clear lines within which to respond to questions. But there are also many more "gray areas" where leaders aren't limited to a single set of answers when approached by reporters, constituents, friends, and others with inquiring minds. Demands for transparency by leaders should be met with a thorough—and frequently personal—consideration before replying to requests for information. That's good advice regardless of who's asking the question and how the answer may be transmitted to others.

Chapter Eight

Learning and Practicing the Art of Listening

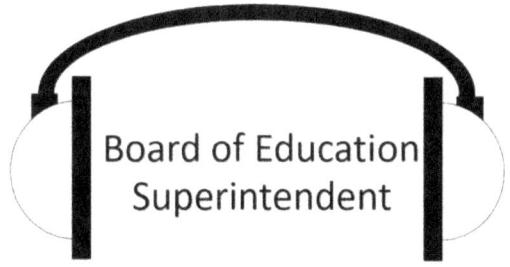

Hearing and listening are seldom the same thing. While the former is easy and can be effective, the latter enables leaders to display the value they give to what others are saying.

One of the main characteristics of a high-performing organization is the leaders' ability to listen to their employees, customers, stakeholders, and community. High-performing boards of education and effective superintendents know the pulse of their communities . . . by listening! Listening is vision critical to all organizations, especially to those organizations that want to be successful in meeting the demands of the people who serve within the organization and the people the organization serves. Too often, organizations focus on public relations, marketing, and conveying a message but fail to include the critical piece of listening to their overall strategy.

Andy Stanley, minister and author, said, "leaders who don't listen will eventually be surrounded by people who have nothing to say." Board members and the superintendent must ensure that listening is the primary component found in their communication strategy. Within any school district in the

United States, the amount of information that must be released to students, faculty, staff, parents/guardians, and the community is massive.

However, the importance of listening far outweighs the need to release information. Think about it: if boards of education and superintendents are not listening to students, faculty, parents, guardians, and the community, how do they disseminate the information they want to know and need? Listening helps the board of education and the superintendent, as a team, focus on communicating the information their community (meaning the school community) wants and needs.

Listening signifies to the person communicating a message that the other person(s) understands and, more important, that they care about and respect the individual who is talking. The board of education and the superintendent, together, must encourage feedback and input from the district's stakeholders. No team can be successful without practicing the art of communication through listening. Think about how powerful listening can be for the board of education and the superintendent. Too many teams—boards of education and their superintendents—never take the time to seek feedback or input, encourage comments, or develop a relationship with stakeholders.

Board members and the superintendent have roles and responsibilities in the community that require interaction with stakeholders. To garner support, which is critical in today's school districts, board members and the superintendent must be accessible to, must be willing to interact with, and, specifically, must listen to stakeholders, who, in many cases, are voters. School boards, including the superintendent, that fail to recognize the importance of listening, accessibility, and keeping stakeholders and the community informed are destined to fail.

Listening goes well beyond listening to stakeholders. For a board of education and superintendent as a team to be effective, listening must be a critical staple within the team's relationship. No matter whether the conversation is positive or negative, words of praise or critique, boards members and superintendents must have a relationship based on mutual trust, which always begins with listening.

As we have mentioned throughout the many chapters, there must a team culture where each voice is welcomed, heard, and valued. In boards where voices are silenced, team members find it difficult to stay focused on their priorities. No matter the issues, boards and the superintendent must remain focused on their goals. If not, the slightest issue can have lasting negative effects. Taking the time to listen to each board member, the superintendent, and stakeholders will prove to be difficult, especially during times of budget cuts, curriculum adoptions, controversy, and political years.

But in reality, it is during these times that more listening and less talking should occur. No one person, board member, or the superintendent has all the answers, which is why a team approach to talking about some of the biggest issues is a no-brainer. Really, listening in difficult times to diverse voices should be a nonnegotiable and is among the strategies of high-performing teams, boards of education, and superintendents.

Valuing listening also helps to keep the district from derailing for the slightest mistake or setback. Mistakes and setbacks are going to occur, no matter what board of education or superintendent that you look at. What sets aside a low-performing board and superintendent from a high-performing board and superintendent is that, when mistakes happen, high-performing boards take the time not only to listen to what happened but also to listen to possible solutions.

Low-performing boards and superintendents are too focused on placing blame and pointing fingers, not about what the next steps are. A culture of listeners lends to a culture of risk-taking, innovation, and stretching the boundaries when it comes to student success. High-performing boards of education and superintendents recognize that focusing on why and next steps is far more productive for students.

PRACTICAL STRATEGIES

- *Create listening opportunities . . . many of them.* Though there are a lot of things to do in a school district, boards of education and the superintendents must make time to listen. Many school districts host districtwide opportunities monthly, like "Coffee with the Superintendent" or "Muffins with Board Members" where stakeholders and constituents have an opportunity, informally, to speak with leaders within the district. Districts that regularly hold these events not only enjoy districtwide support but also create an empowering district culture that sends the message that every voice is critical to the district's mission.
- *Designate time for each board member to speak.* Many boards of education utilize committee structures to empower each board member to concentrate on items that they are interested in pursuing, learning more about, or discussing. Furthermore, many boards of education allow each member time at the biweekly or monthly board meeting to speak briefly about their topics of choice, ask questions, and speak about their interactions with stakeholders since the last board meeting. Though this may scare some boards and superintendents, this is a great strategy to empower each board

member to be part of the district's mission. Though many would think the board member would speak about things that are not relevant to the district's vision or speak about things that are not in the board's purview, board members understand that their few minutes are important so they really take the time to speak about things that impact the entire district, not just some random item that would not be of interest to others.

- *Focus on the signal, not the ground noise.* Though board members and the superintendent will have differing opinions from time to time, both need to focus on the signal, not necessarily the ground noise. What this means is that, when differing opinions happen and disagreements occur, listen to what is truly trying to be said. Overwhelming each board member and the superintendent is trying to do what is right and create the best opportunities for each student. With this understanding, there has to be some give and take, not focusing on some of the most outlandish ideas or remarks, but what they are truly all about. One slipup doesn't mean a board member is an obstructionist in regard to transforming the district, neither is the superintendent the devil by speaking the truth. Board members and superintendents must focus on action, the votes, the deeds, and not necessarily what is being said in the heat of the moment. By the way, board members and superintendents are human and will most definitely make mistakes from time to time.

KEY TAKEAWAY

Taking the time to listen more and talk less is a dying art when it comes to leaders. We see local, state, and national leaders who are more focused on talking than they are focused on listening to the opposing side. Those on the opposite side of the debate or table can bring great value to the discussion, though sadly they are silenced in many board rooms, offices, and communities. Board members and superintendents can transform a district's culture or ignite the engine to greater success by just making the time to listen to stakeholders.

No matter if the feedback is good, bad, or ugly, when stakeholders recognize that a board of education and superintendent is accessible and open to feedback, they feel empowered and more engaged in the direction of the district. Though just listening will not solve all of the district's problems or create better outcomes for students, listening, always, is the first step to greater things to happen in any organization!

Chapter Nine

Socially Speaking

Online Engagement Matters

> *An active presence on social media has moved from luxury to necessity in public education. Leaders can choose how active they want to be, but everyone can be an important player online.*

When the Pew Research Center began tracking Americans' engagement on social media in 2005, it estimated barely 5 percent of those 18–65+ were engaged. By 2019, Pew analysts estimated more than 7 in every 10 adults were regular users of one or more social media sites such as YouTube, Instagram, Snapchat, Twitter, and Facebook. Almost universally, social media use rates continue to grow.

What this means for superintendents and school board members is simple: the overwhelming majority of your stakeholders—employees, students, parents, community leaders, and other constituents—are active on social media. School leaders who themselves want to exercise maximum impact of their communications efforts are going to be engaged on social media—in one platform or another, to one degree or another.

Among other reasons, school leaders explore social media engagement in order to

- share positive messages about activities within the district,
- grow public understanding of actions by district leaders,
- increase public support for public education,
- remain in touch with community conversations relating to the district, and
- ensure a district message "presence" where those discussions occur.

As chief communications officer for the district, superintendents may be more frequently active on social media. But there are plenty of reasons—and options—for board members to be socially engaged as well.

SUPERINTENDENT SIGNALS

The role of the superintendent in communicating via social media is somewhat tricky. No matter if the superintendent states, "comments are my own views and do not reflect that of the district or board of education," they do. The superintendent must be very careful not to engage too much in political debate—particularly political debate that is political-party specific. Though many will not agree with this view, we contend that the superintendent is the spokesperson of the board, and when the superintendent speaks, the general public assumes the comments are endorsed by the board of education—no matter if the social media profile is personal or professional.

The best rule of thumb is for the superintendent to be guarded when using social media. Some of the most effective superintendents always advocate for students' needs but do it in a way that does not offend board members, legislators, and other elected leaders of a particular political party. Furthermore, effective superintendents use communication—face-to-face, on social media, in interviews, and press releases—to engage stakeholders, not to isolate stakeholders. Stay neutral, positive, and board supportive on social media. Educate yourself on issues and have someone, including the board chair, read your social media post should you have concerns about neutrality of the post. For hot topics or political topics, see if the board, board chair, or board attorney supports the post.

But situations happen where we see superintendents publicly say something on social media, in an e-mail, or in a press release that ends up offending or targeting individuals, or mistakenly communicates inaccurate information. Not surprisingly, we see more and more superintendents and boards of education whose relationships end up being damaged because of social media or ill-advised communiqués.

BOARD MEMBERS PICK DEGREES OF ENGAGEMENT

We know school board members who vary vastly in their level of engagement on social media, including those who don't use any platform for any reason. Of course, there also are board members who, like some superintendents, actively post on Facebook, Twitter, Instagram, and other pages on a daily basis.

One beauty of social media use by school board members lies with that very degree of personal choice for frequency of activity. There are three obvious alternatives, which we have identified as "monitoring," "promoting," and "engaging." Each option builds on the earlier one in terms of time involved, capacity to communicate messages, and ability to engage others using the specific social media platform.

Monitoring

"Monitoring" board members begin by creating an official social media page on their platform of choice. Facebook and/or Twitter are recommended as starting points that will allow, if desired, greater engagement in one of the subsequent options. "Monitoring" board members are for the most part observers.

They principally follow (Twitter) or friend (Facebook) the similar social media pages of the district and its schools. Other pages they may track are those of board colleagues, booster clubs, local governments, C of C and like organizations, and key education resources such as the state education department, national and state education advocacy groups, and other sources of K–12 information.

This "monitoring" approach principally enables school board members to be aware of the information being placed on social media by others. When appropriate, board members may want to share what they have gleaned with other district leaders.

Promoting

"Promoting" board members possess all of the social media communications routes of "monitoring" and opportunities to build upon them. Social media pages maintained by board members choosing the "promoting" approach will be more active—both in terms of the time spent engaged and the interaction with other social media users. One decision to be made is the degree to which "promoting" board members want that interaction to take place.

Social media pages may be established so that only you—as the operator/manager—may post information. Others may view your posts but may not react nor make their own posts to your page. However, such an approach severely limits the use of the page to gain feedback. Another choice would be to allow only "friends" or "followers" to react and/or post to your page. This approach allows you to permit, delete, or otherwise limit what others may say on your page.

That's an important consideration as it's doubtful any board members would want to create a social media outlet that gives critics or spreaders of disinformation a venue for placing negative posts about the district. Take note: Like it or not, debate is one of the principal functions of social media. An honest exchange of ideas on social media is no different from expressions of diverse viewpoints in any other forum.

"Promoting" board members have multiple opportunities to spread the word about positive district messages. By "sharing" (Facebook) or "retweeting" (Twitter) posts from others' pages, board members can reach a larger audience with good news about the district. The same can be said for reposting useful information to parents and other stakeholders from a wide variety of online resources. Greater degrees of posting and sharing activity by "promoting" board members also mean the potential of increasing followers and friends who return to their pages for information.

Engaging

"Engaging" board members can achieve all the social media activities of "monitoring" and "promoting" board members . . . and, if they wish, go to the next level.

For example, "engaging" board members will be creators of their own messages for purposes such as gathering feedback. This can be an extremely beneficial way of using social media to gauge constituent sentiment ahead of a key vote. In order to most effectively use social media to gain input, users must promote the availability of the question. Alert friends and followers of a poll or question. And above all, let your readers know what you learned from their input. Don't ask and then fail to tell how you benefited from their responses.

"Engaging" board members should be prepared for the "engagement" of followers and friends. This will require more of your time to monitor your social media page. That's not to say that every post or comment requires a response on your part. But maximizing the value of a social media page means paying attention to the activity therein.

Of course, "engaging" board members also will be faced with choices about dealing with critics. Again, false information may be deleted, but exchanges involving honest differences of opinion are often important in leaders' decision-making process. But "engaging" board members also have a platform for sharing the facts with their followers and friends.

Arguments on social media seldom produce a win for the other side, and they even less frequently change the opinion of those on either side of an issue. But school leaders who use social media to share additional facts, reasons for decisions, alternatives, and factors that diminish those choices strengthen the quality of the conversation with constituents. When it comes to social media use, school leaders may go small or go large. There is value in all levels of engagement. It's your choice!

PRACTICAL STRATEGIES

- *Communicate to drive the conversation.* At no other time in the history of the modern age of education has there been so many opportunities for boards of education and superintendents to communicate. Social media allows boards of education and superintendents to easily drive the conversation in education. A quick search on Facebook, Twitter, and LinkedIn shows thousands of school districts, individual board members, and superintendents who are active in the area of social media.

    This is a good thing. This presence of educators and board members allows them the avenue to drive the conversation. The key is to be active on social media. A rule of thumb is to post or repost new content, share content, or like messages on a daily basis. Do not go weeks or months without posting or sharing information.
- *Engage with the community—positively.* A rule of thumb is to never engage in the negative posts; instead, only share correct information. The goal of being active on social media is for members of the boards of education and superintendents to share information. Applaud the positives, share correct information, and devalue misinformation. Never engage in personal back and forth, but acknowledge constituents' feedback and share information that can help educate and inform constituents.
- *Leverage social media to garner support.* Today's rapid speed of news and easy access to quick information makes the use of social media critical in school districts across the nation. Boards of education and superintendents must recognize that most of the community is now getting news and information from social media. To garner community support, boards of education and superintendents must have a regular and active presence in the social media universe. Use social media not only to keep the community informed but also to gain their support. The key is to maintain a regular and active presence.

KEY TAKEAWAY

If school districts are not active in the social media universe, they are likely missing a large portion of their constituents. Whether we like it or not, social media is a permanent and growing tool in any school district's communication strategy. Boards of education and superintendents must use social media not only to keep the community informed but also to garner their support. The key is to maintain an active presence in the social media universe but keep the information transparent, timely, targeted, and accurate. School boards and superintendents are not on social media just to say they are but, instead, to actually use it to educate and inform the community, with the goal of garnering their support for the district's mission.

Chapter Ten

Putting the Forward Focus on Growth

Board of Education
Superintendent

> *Improvement is a never-ending target in education. Measurements—test scores, employee pay, facility upgrades, budget balancing—represent key points leaders must convey to stakeholders.*

To be clear, the vast majority of public schools in the United States are doing an amazing job. Student achievement, student opportunities, and student readiness have never been higher in the history of the modern-day public school. Graduation rates continue to set all-time records every year over the past decade. The reason is the countless hours that dedicated stakeholders—including board members and superintendents—put into their work. Though the majority of schools are doing well, there is always room for improvement and for growth.

When school board members take office, much of their knowledge—and thus their attention—is on what has transpired in the district in its recent past. Too often, there is a tendency to focus on what occurred 3, 5, and even 10 years ago. Quickly, though, new school leaders discover they must emphasize the future to move the district forward 3, 5, and 10 years down the road.

Communication is key for school districts to continually grow. Board members and the superintendent set the tone in the district. If they have a forward vision, then others, too, will focus on the future. However, if board members and the superintendent cannot overcome the past or get shackled to the present, stakeholders likewise will also focus on the past and present. Jack Welch, former CEO of General Electric, said it best, "A leader's job is to look into the future and see the organization, not as it is, but as it should be." Many times, boards of education and superintendents try to address issues from the past and never can come together to address the present.

As we have mentioned repeatedly throughout this book, stakeholders and constituents hang on every word from board members and the superintendent. The power of words cannot be underestimated, especially in today's schools. Faced with unbelievable odds of success, school districts must have a strategic focus and plan to overcome some "Goliath" obstacles, issues, and barriers. Like in any situation, we argue that communication is the secret ingredient to helping any board of education and superintendent push through the obstacles and dismantle the chains that often hold districts back from creating the best experiences and opportunities for students.

The effectiveness of the board's communication strategy, typically carried out by the superintendent, will help the district continue to focus on the horizon. There are many districts, nationwide, that have unlocked the code to a forward focus. When looking for these forward-focused districts, look for a strategic social media campaign, a district brand, regular use of town hall or community meetings, a concise communication strategy, and press releases with multiple board members and the superintendent speaking with one voice. This laser focus on the team and the future results in huge dividends for not only students but also the community and the team of board members and the superintendent.

When the board of education and superintendent understand and recognize the power of communication on the district's strategy, the engine to change begins to purr like a brand-new Chevrolet Corvette that just rolled off the assembly line in Bowling Green, Kentucky. Everything that is communicated relates back to "why the district is focused on student achievement 3, 5, and 10 years into the future." Though current district occurrences are important, the most important thing to keep in mind, as a board member and superintendent, is how current issues, trends, and concerns impact the district's long-term goal and vision.

Through a strategic communication strategy, the board of education and superintendent are changing the course of the district. Focused words of inspiration, empowerment, and inclusivity must be present in the district's communication with stakeholders. Board members and the superintendent, through communication, are seeking to garner support from stakeholders, to be part of the journey, while also informing stakeholders to be better equipped to be active and productive members of the district's team. Yes, through a precise communication strategy, the board of education and superintendent can amass an army of stakeholders for support to grow the district.

PRACTICAL STRATEGIES

- *Look toward the horizon.* Board members and superintendents must focus on what students will need 3, 5, and 10 years into the future. Though current student needs are important and must be addressed, what is the district doing about what students will need in the future to be successful? The team—board members and the superintendent—can multitask, addressing current needs while also putting in place things for the future. The key here is not to get overwhelmed by what is currently happening or what the current needs are so that you fail to plant the seeds for future harvests.
- *Communicate empowerment.* The roles of the board and superintendent are extremely challenging and rewarding. Both roles are extremely lonely; however, neither position needs to be. To grow the district strategically, there must be a concerted team effort not only by the board and the superintendent but also by stakeholders. No matter the size of the team of board members and superintendent, stakeholders must be empowered to be the 12th man on the field to help move the district forward. Empowerment always leads to greater things within an organization. Communication is critical to creating a culture of empowerment within the team and district. There cannot be empowerment without trust, transparency, and unmuted voices.
- *Take risks.* Growth will never occur in organizations that are complacent, content with the status quo, happy with today's results. Board members and the superintendent must communicate to stakeholders that growth is expected and calculated and strategic risks are encouraged. The board of education and the superintendent have considerable influence on the district culture. High-performing boards of education and superintendents are fixated on growth and innovation in their school districts. Not only do they expect to be the best now, but they expect to be the best in the future. In terms of "best," they expect to be the best at offering state-of-the-art facilities, instruction, experiences, and opportunities to students. They communicate the expectation that anything but first place is not acceptable and

empower others to carry out the mission of making sure that every student has the best quality education possible.

KEY TAKEAWAY

Growth is often overlooked in organizations. Remember Blackberry, the cell phone with the keyboard that took the world by storm. As Blackberry was dominant for so long, they failed to think about growth or focus on new user trends, which opened the door for Apple's iPhone and others. If organizations become complacent, failure is almost certain. Board members and superintendents must always look toward the horizon.

What are signs the fig leaves are showing? What will students' needs, goals, and aspirations look like 3, 5, and 10 years into the future? Effective growth is always proactive, not reactive. Waiting until change needs to occur always puts organizations and teams behind the "eight ball." Board members and superintendents must always have their "fingers on the pulse" of the needs, goals, and aspirations of their students so that they initiate change, which will result in growth before it's too late.

Chapter Eleven

Building and Maintaining Support for Schools

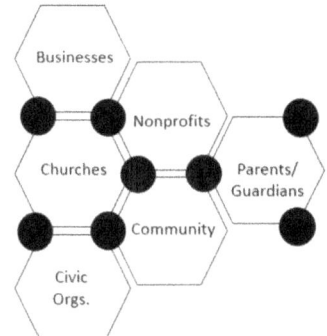

Major decisions often elicit major reactions. Effective leaders not only explain how they arrived at a conclusion but also how they respect the input of stakeholders passionate about issues.

In 1999, two armed students killed 12 classmates and a teacher at Columbine High School in Colorado. Over 20 years, the phrase "Columbine-like" became synonymous with planned school shootings. The school became a sort of morbid tourist stopping point. In 2019, seeing no end to the "morbid fascination," the superintendent and school board proposed a bold response—demolition of the structure where the killings took place and construction of a new school at a cost of up to $70 million. But first, they began what the superintendent called "a conversation with the community."

Fortunately, few district leaders face monumental decisions on a scale similar to their Colorado counterparts. Yet virtually all superintendents and school board members with any significant length of service will be challenged by major choices for the direction of their districts—closing existing schools or relocating new facilities, the fate of academic programs, staffing during shrinking resource periods, and even the selection of new leaders.

While there can be no panacea of process guaranteeing success in all cases, school leaders can put themselves in the best possible position by building support through communications right from the start. And that begins with a mentality of visible listening—to the community at large and target audiences who will be impacted by the ultimate action.

TALKING UP MAJOR INITIATIVES

Regardless of the necessity of any major decision faced by school leaders—for example, a dangerously aging building—there will be people with differing reactions to the options for resolution. That's why it is essential that the process begins with an earnest, two-pronged approach to building that support—education about the issue and listening to feedback. Placing the facts of the decision to be made before stakeholders may sound like a no-brainer.

But too many communications campaigns begin and end there, in a sort of "tell them and let them choose" approach. While this method isn't guaranteed to fail, it leaves much to chance. A stronger plan marries A-1 (explaining the problem and the choices) with A-2 (a formal plan for gathering input). They should be conducted simultaneously to demonstrate both the importance of the pending decision and the importance that decision makers are placing on stakeholder response.

For years, a community meeting or a series of public forums were the primary tools for such ventures by district leaders. And they still are effective options today. But the internet and social media have added online surveys to the mix—an option that has grown greatly in recent years. Effective online surveys accomplish three things: they underscore the promise of seeking feedback, provide input in a speedy and inexpensive way, and can give decision makers a look at what support—or opposition—there is to the possibilities on the table.

While the educating and listening phase is going on, school leaders need not be sitting around and waiting. This is the time to be encouraging supporters to become vocal about the issue. Prominent community "opinion leaders" are invaluable external voices ahead of the final voting on the matter. Teams of district personnel and supporters can address local civic organizations—

and not just the PTAs and PTOs. The reality is that the educational effort may add some listeners to your side while also silencing some potential critics when given the facts early on in the process.

District leaders' communications are vital throughout the process. Keeping the district "family"—employees, parents, backers—in the know feeds the fact-based opinions they in turn will share with their own circles of influence. A school custodian, an aide, or a bus driver have the same capacity to share information with family and friends as do a superintendent, a board member, or a principal.

A surge of public support—no matter how large or small—is an asset in any major campaign by district leaders to achieve or to change or to advance toward a desired goal. Communications early and often can be just as critical to eventual success as is the strength of the underlying facts of the issue at the outset.

MAKING A CASE FOR TAXES

How school boards and superintendents acquire local resources for education is a surprising mixture of routes from state to state. In Tennessee, for example, school boards must ask the county government to allocate funds. In Ohio, some years there are nearly 100 school tax referendums on the ballot. In Kentucky, school taxes can be raised—and even lowered—and still require three separate budget actions by local school boards.

Each of these examples represents a necessary part of funding education, but they also embody a function of school leadership that requires effective communications to be successful. Even in a time of economic growth, tax opponents are an increasingly vocal—and organized—force boards and superintendents ignore at their peril. Much as with the major initiatives addressed earlier in this chapter, the annual process of going to voters or other public officials for money compels local education leaders to have a message and a way of getting that out.

Well before a school board has a hearing on the upcoming budget, the administration should be making presentations at board meetings on the district's fiscal condition and factors that will impact the budget. In short, the time to talk about the need for more money is *before the talk is about how much more money.*

Here are some points to consider:

- First, give the public examples of what the district did with the money it provided in the current fiscal year. New computers, replacement band uniforms, additional media center study materials, more energy efficient

buildings, and buses just begin a truly endless list. And if you have taken steps in the past year that have reduced costs, never let that information slide by without having attention—in detail—brought to bear.
- Next, share the external factors that drive school and district expenses. People may not like it, but they understand that food, electricity, gasoline, and insurance are costs of everyday life. Don't skirt around the issue of personnel costs. Teachers, librarians, secretaries, and their colleagues are the family members, friends, and neighbors of your taxpayers. Retaining quality classroom educators—and the support staff necessary to run the schools—is a cost of doing the business of educating children.
- Discuss your options. What will happen if you hold the line on salaries and benefits, if you don't upgrade technology, if you leave the roof on for another year, if you don't replace buses as recommended? What can be accomplished with the additional revenues—specifically—if you do raise taxes? What examples can you show demonstrating your district's efficient use of resources in the past as a foundation for what taxpayers can expect in the coming year?
- Now assemble your talking points in a combination of all three of these discussions. Include them as a regular part of your explanation for the basis of your tax rate deliberations. Make your case for what the kids need in the classroom!

SELECTING A SUPERINTENDENT

An excellent case can be made that the defining decision for any school board member is the outcome of a search for a new chief executive officer for the district. There is no more crucial action setting the future direction of a school district than the hiring of a new superintendent. And honest, transparent communications by the board—and its individual members—is an essential element of any search.

Faced with a change at the top of the district leadership chain of command—whether by retirement, replacement, or other reason—school boards are challenged to reassert their own collective abilities to act in the best interest of their students, their employees, and their communities. There always will be second guessers, regardless of the outcome of the search. Boards can minimize the impact of detractors not only by how they conduct the search but also by how they convey their intent of the process.

Whether using a search consultant or going it alone, a board in superintendent search mode is advised to include early on some process of asking stakeholders what characteristics they give high importance to in a new top administrator. Previous superintendent experience? Intimate knowledge of the community? Knowledge specific to an ongoing challenge facing the district? A demonstrated capacity of leadership demonstrated in current and earlier jobs? A homegrown candidate over "an outsider"? Simple public forums or an online survey can accomplish this and exhibit that visible listening discussed earlier in this chapter.

Clear and consistent messages about the selection process should be maintained throughout. An outline of the process, including time line, search specifics, and other pertinent information can be posted on the district's website.

What is not said can be just as important as what is said during the search. Individual board members should never champion a candidate—even in private conversations. Nor should a board member express opinion of a belief—for example, favoring a local candidate—that might dissuade interested hopefuls to withdraw.

Finally, when the vote comes, board members should do no more nor less than they would in explaining their "yea" or "nay" on any other important action. Obviously, a united board is a help to a new superintendent. But even a member who voted in the minority on the decision can assist the new leader by making it clear she or he will work affirmatively with the district's next superintendent. Board members can accompany the new CEO to civic meetings or school events or even just walking around town. Visible signs of support after the vote can be just as endorsing as a "yes" vote at the action meeting.

PRACTICAL STRATEGIES

- *Think community*. When communicating, the board of education and the superintendent must keep the community in mind. The community is the purpose of all messaging. The message must be targeted to each community—based on understanding, beliefs, and other demographics. This means that the message must be tailored and community specific: what works in one district may not work in another district. Though using another district's strategy is acceptable and encouraged, always make sure that the messaging is community specific.
- *Develop a communication plan.* Communication plans are increasingly becoming a necessity in school districts across the nation. Describing how communication will happen, communication plans help keep the messaging on target. The key to developing an effective communication plan is to involve the community. Organize a diverse communication committee, with community members, educators, and administrators. Allow the community

to help guide how the board of education and superintendent communicate a collective, specific, strategic, and clear message.
- *Define key roles and involve experts.* The district's communication requires that everyone understands their roles. No board member or superintendent should be ahead of the collective message of the board or the district. In most cases, the superintendent or board chair is the voice of the board of education. Nothing says dysfunctional more than individual board members delivering different messages ahead of the overall board or district message.

There can't be different messages to the community. Keep in mind that community support is contingent upon a clear message. If the community receives different messages, who are they to believe? Furthermore, the board or superintendent may struggle with messaging involving public relations experts or others. It is better to recognize problems early than to communicate poorly or ineffectively with the community. Boards of education and superintendents often have one time to get the message out to the community. Rarely are there opportunities for "do overs." Seek help early and as often as possible to make sure that the message is on target and transparent.

KEY TAKEAWAY

Understand the purpose of communicating with constituents. Communication is not only about keeping constituents informed but also about garnering their support. Boards of education and superintendents often mistake communication as a means to only keep constituents informed. Though informed constituents often lead to support, when communicating garners support it results in full support.

School districts across the nation today need more support than ever before. To accomplish support, districts and boards of education must have a clear, collaborative, and strategic message. Think about what information your constituents need to support the district, then deliver it using a message that is tailored, targeted, and transparent. Cookie-cutter messages rarely garner the level of support needed to create change in any organization.

Boards of education and superintendents, together, are facing incredible odds. To overcome the many obstacles and roadblocks and to ensure the focus remains on student success, community support is vision critical. The community, in most cases, does not just freely provide support; it expects the school district to earn support. School districts do this by keeping the community informed, up to date, and involved, and all of this is accomplished through a clear message.

Chapter Twelve

Success

See it, Speak it

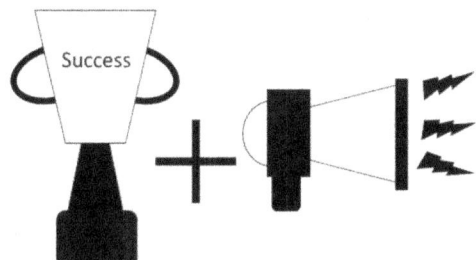

Leaders aren't trained to be modest nor should they be. Negatives often outnumber positives, so observances of true accomplishments aren't just an opportunity, they're a responsibility.

Truly amazing things happen daily in America's public schools but, too often, are overshadowed by challenges: a leaking roof, a discipline incident, a staff dispute. The public can become fixated on those challenges if school leaders fail to effectively communicate the good news. And that means celebrating more than student test scores. Improved student achievement is Job 1, but Job 2 continues each district's task list.

Sadly, too many public schools, boards of education, and superintendents have fallen victim to determining effectiveness by test scores. When this happens, we quantify a system of accountability based overwhelmingly on scores, with little credence to the other powerful things happening throughout the district. When we talk about successes, naturally, people automatically assume that we are talking about student test scores. Though student test scores are important, based on the era of high-stakes testing throughout the nation, test scores are only one component to a district's scorecard.

Did we mention there are amazing things happening in school districts, many things? Unfortunately, many boards of education and superintendents fail to publicize all of the successes of the team. Boards of education and superintendents must be able to communicate more than just recent success with student test scores. Think about the many things that boards of education and superintendents do that go well beyond test scores.

In districts where boards of education can set their own tax rates or can pass school bonds, think about the impact the money used from successfully increasing revenue will have on the district overall. Increasing taxes or passing a school bond can take months of campaigning, marketing, and interacting one-on-one with constituents. If successful, the board and superintendent must publicize their success.

Many board members and the superintendent will have difficulty talking about success as they do not like to brag and are humble leaders. We would argue that, as a team, you are celebrating success as a team, not individual member success. As a team, you can still celebrate success while also being humble.

Communicate how the team worked together to pass a school bond, increase teacher pay, or provide students more access to the arts, or how the board reduced class size or even completed a school renovation on time and under budget. No matter the success, communicate the work of the board and the superintendent, as a team, that resulted in a positive outcome for the district and for students.

In today's era of public scrutiny of public education, more pressures, and the call for more accountability, boards of education and superintendents must be able and willing to communicate a positive message. Like other organizations and teams that face negative odds of success, boards of education and superintendents must be out front sharing how the district is succeeding. They must be proactive and not reactive. Our suggestion is that communicating success, like other team communications, must be strategic.

Boards of education and superintendents must be able to connect the dots; they must show how the district achieved success (by celebrating the team) and how any success of the board and the superintendent equals student success. The more the board of education and superintendent can relate their success to student success, the more stakeholders will appreciate their efforts.

Keep in mind, boards of education, superintendents, teachers, staff members, and the district overall can only experience success when students experience success. Boards of education and superintendents who believe that they can only succeed when students succeed experience far more successes as a team, and they are far more productive in their roles.

At the end of the day, board members and the superintendent, like everyone else, want to succeed in their roles. When they do succeed for students, they must not be afraid to communicate those successes, no matter the size or shape of the win. John Maxwell, the best-selling author, minister, and leadership coach, says, "A profile of a winning team—they play to win. They have a winning attitude. They keep improving. They make their teammates more successful." As boards and superintendents experience success, they must not only communicate their wins but also communicate continuous success.

Communicating success provides the board of education and the superintendent an opportunity to stress the importance of continuous improvement and growth, which will lead to even more successful outcomes for the district and students. By doing so, boards of education and the superintendent can challenge stakeholders not to become complacent, satisfied with the win, but eager to climb another mountain and accomplish even more as a team. Don't be afraid to use today's success as the engine for greater things for the team, the district, and students.

PRACTICAL STRATEGIES

- *Visually communicate success.* Boards of education and the superintendent should visually show district successes. Keep a scorecard on the district's website, in the district office, in the boardroom, and in every school to show stakeholders what has been accomplished and other goals. Stakeholders like visuals that are easy to read, colorful, and easy to access.
- *Celebrate/communicate by saying thank you.* In many cases, communicating success has a lot to do with how you say it. Though there is nothing wrong with celebrating team success, many boards of education and superintendents may find it difficult to brag a little about their team. A strategy is to celebrate the work of others—while also celebrating the board's and superintendent's success. For example, celebrate by thanking taxpayers for voting for the tax rate hike or school bond by releasing a "Thank You" memo or flyer. You are thanking others, but you also are celebrating the success. This can be done with a lot of things in a school district—start by thanking others but also bring attention to a recent success.

- *Make success part of the district's brand.* Boards of education and superintendents must make success, winning, part of the team's and district's brand. No one else is going to communicate the district's successes. Just like other winning teams and organizations, school districts must communicate success so that others believe that the board of education and superintendent are effective in their governance and leadership and that they are all about winning for students.
- *Be strategic: Help to keep successes fresh in everyone's mind.* Developing a communication strategy that outlines, in detail, when and how to release information is critical to communicating team successes and milestones. A communication strategy helps publicize successes in a way that is not overkill but just enough to help remind everyone of the team's effectiveness and ability to win for students. Over-publicizing the board's and superintendent's successes can damage the team's brand, so the need for an overall strategy is critical to the team's approach.
- *Communicate success in terms people understand.* Too often, education publications and marketing campaigns are plagued by educational jargon that the general public simply doesn't understand. The easiest way to celebrate success is to relate success back to students and, in many cases, the local community. Show how the success has led to increases in student achievement, more student scholarships, more student college admission. Also, when it pertains to taxes or school bonds, show how the district has pumped more money into the local economy, which leads to more local jobs, among other things.

KEY TAKEAWAY

"Success" is not a bad word. Boards of education and superintendents are doing amazing things, and those successes that are resulting in student success must be celebrated, recognized, and communicated. For whatever reason, many of the district's successes escape the public—never seeing the light of day or being overlooked. Boards of education and superintendents, as a team necessity in today's climate, must ensure that successes are consistently made public and accessible to the public.

One of the biggest mistakes boards of education and superintendents make when communicating is that they think communication occurred. Often, success in education is not clearly communicated. Boards of education and superintendents need to take the time to develop a clear winning message that speaks about successes. Regular messages of successes are a great strategy to keep the district and community focused on winning. We see it all the time, the school districts communicating positive messages only during times of struggle. Boards of education and school districts, without overkill, should be regularly communicating all the positives that are happening in the district—not only when something goes wrong.

A regular, timely, and consistent messaging strategy will not only help celebrate the positives in the district but also the community is more likely to see the message as believable. Social media has provided districts and boards of education free tools to message that take seconds to reach constituents. Use social media wisely and often, but the key is to use it—period. More and more, parents and community members are receiving their news from social media—and less by press releases on websites and in newspapers. Boards of education and superintendents are encouraged to utilize the simple forms of communication that social media provides.

Chapter Thirteen

Communicating in a Timely Manner in Calm and in Crisis

Keeping stakeholders in the know is a year-round exercise, but it's especially true when leaders deal with a crisis. Good engagement practices used at other times prove themselves again.

Life teaches that timing isn't always everything. But timing one's message—the right words at the right time—almost always will enhance the impact of those words. And the timing of school leaders' messages should be part of their planning to reach—and to influence—their audiences. It's natural to equate the importance of a message with the level of calamity of a situation. In a crisis, clear, accurate information is essential. However, communicating effectively in a crisis should be just as much an extension of careful message planning for the routine days as for the times that raise blood pressures.

For example, every spring, high school guidance counselors can calculate the total dollars in college scholarships earned by that year's graduating class. That data could be passed around administrative channels simply in one sentence in an update to the principal. Yet, savvy school administrators are learning that announcing such a level of achievement as a part of the graduation season frequently results in heightened attention to what those graduating seniors have accomplished. Timing!

Have you ever read or viewed a feature story about a college or university graduate-to-be with an amazing tale of triumph over adversity? Institutions of higher education have learned that reporters are looking for stories that differentiate this year's graduation even from those of past years, so they seek out such examples and alert the media. That student's success story would have been just as true weeks earlier, but the upcoming graduation makes it relevant now. Again, timing!

ROUTINE CAN BE NOTEWORTHY

It's a fact! The overwhelming majority of local news media outlets are going to do back-to-school stories every fall. Of course, school leaders must give out essential, annual facts of calendars, start times, enrollment, bus routes, and such. But they also can and should use this opportunity of assured media—and stakeholder—interest to draw attention to the new and different for the upcoming year.

A few thoughts for back-to-school communications:

- Always give "the family"—district and school employees—information about changes for the new school year. They are vital members of your communications team as friends, neighbors, and visible representatives in the community. They don't have to be able to answer all questions, but they should be sufficiently in the know to be able to get a parent needing more information to the right person or unit. And there will be more employees who will appreciate the extra knowledge than those who will complain about another e-mail or memo from the board.
- Share "change," but sell "expansion": There always will be different aspects from one school year to the next; it's a given of the business of education, and even though the information should be shared, it can be a "ho-hum" message. But when a school or district is doing something more for students and/or staff, that's more of an "oh, really?" message. Having a new school nurse is one thing but having new health offerings available to students is much more of a story. Bus routes probably change from year

to year, but having new vehicle tracking technology or expanded security camera units are a different matter.
- It's a sad reality, but safety improvements now—and going forward for the foreseeable future—are going to be of interest on a widespread basis. From new technologies to specialist training for staff, from more counselors and school safety officers to tightened building access, these will get noticed by parents, students, staff, and the public at large. There is one caveat here: Don't oversell improved safety to the extent that the message is schools aren't already safe places to learn and work. It's important to demonstrate attention to safety, but improved school security shouldn't be the only thing you highlight ahead of the start of classes.
- Schools actually have two "back to" seasons. The start of the second semester of the year each January is another opportunity to talk about new services and programs. And early January often is a slow news period for local media outlets. Help them fill their respective news needs by pitching these story options right after the holiday season ends.

Consider that July and August board meetings can provide excellent forums for spreading the word about what's going to be new for the upcoming year. This can be accomplished with presentations to the board or simple reports that can be posted to district and school social media and websites. These create information resources for staff, families, and the news media alike. And they can enable board members themselves to be better informed and able to help tell the stories across the community.

IN A CRISIS: WHAT YOU SAY AND WHEN YOU SAY IT MATTERS

Who Talks to the Media?

Just as there is no universal definition of "crisis" for schools and/or districts, there can be no single advice on "best practices" for school leaders about communicating when a crisis happens. Entire books and lengthy seminars have been devoted to this subject. However, a fundamental component of any crisis response plan is to be prepared to ensure a timely response to any situation that arises.

Remember: In a crisis, there are *always* steps being taken to resolve the situation, and there are *always* things that can be shared about that activity. Not all the details. Not answers to all the questions. But even when the primary ongoing activity is to investigate and gather information, to protect and ensure student safety and to determine appropriate next steps, there *always* is information about every crisis that can be communicated by district leaders.

It should be noted by board members that crisis communications should be a responsibility of the superintendent and her/his response team. One function of that team is to keep the members of the board informed and understanding what can—and what cannot—be shared with others. Board members should expect to be kept in the know and, when called upon to take action, to be provided with sufficient information needed to do so. But delivering information *in the middle of an ongoing crisis situation*—including deciding what is shared in those messages to the media and the public—needs to be handled by the professional staff acting on the latest and best information for appropriate responses.

What to Say and When to Say It

- When first confronted with a school-related crisis—and a demand for immediate response—stress what steps are being taken to ensure student and staff safety, how information on the status of the situation is being gathered, and what agencies (if any) are assisting with the crisis response. Set a tentative timetable for updating the information, noting a final timetable will be made (if necessary) in consultation with emergency responders.
- Once you have sufficient facts to assess the situation, start crafting your message by considering what you can say, as opposed to beginning with "We can't say this" or "We can't say that." It will be easier to focus on what you want to communicate by settling on the things you can talk about. Then work on the basis/reasoning for being unable to provide information on anticipated questions.
- Craft a written statement with the facts you can release. Briefly explain issues that cannot be addressed at this time. Note: You don't have to completely limit yourself to the written statement, but it increases your ability to focus interested parties on the facts you can release. Make sure the same written statement is available online, posted on social media, and distributed to key members of the administrative team and all board members.
- If the crisis involves student safety, conduct an initial family briefing apart from a session with news media. Set up a process for parents to get their updates (with a different information access option for reporters).
- If new information shows an earlier official release was in error, issue a corrected statement as soon as possible. There is no need to assess blame; it was the best information available at the time. But be as sure as you can that the new information is correct in all respects.

Rumor-Driving Crises

Social media has raised the number of rumor-driven headaches for school leaders, but there is still plenty of staff-spread misinformation in schools and districts. Don't think for a second these can't rise to a full-blown crisis; in fact, response experts in the field often refer to these as "smoldering" crises.

School leaders faced with worrisome rumors will first want to determine whether the matter is even worth their time in pursuing further. One school communications pro calls this task "figuring out whether the issue has legs." Are you hearing about this from multiple people? Is there enough validity to the subject to merit concerns? Is there a real downside to simply letting time go by and seeing what develops? This is especially true regarding rumors on social media. Are enough different people sharing, commenting, and creating a degree of uproar that requires looking into the issue further?

Clearly, some rumors are of themselves a priority for review—claims of inappropriate student-staff activities, allegations of criminal activities, threats of dangerous acts. The potential repercussions of failing to act about such rumors are too risky to chance. This doesn't mean that there ultimately will be a need to communicate anything to anyone, except perhaps internally among the district leadership team.

An additional trouble with an actual "smoldering" crisis is that often someone at the management level could have or should have become aware of the situation. That doubles down on the superintendent's decisions: how to deal with the rumor and whether someone should have acted more quickly. This isn't always so much about disciplinary decisions as much as determining if changes in practices or procedures are necessary.

PRACTICAL STRATEGIES

- *Communicate.* Too often, boards of education and superintendents are not communicating about the good or the bad. Today's world and the craving of information necessitates that boards of education and superintendents communicate with the community—their constituents. It is surprising to see how sporadic many school districts and boards of education are in sharing information on their websites, on social media, and in the local news. To be active in the educational arena, boards of education and superintendents must communicate often and accurately.
- *Preparation.* In today's world, there is no district that can be too prepared. Every board of education and school district should have a board-approved communication plan. Within the communication plan, there should be clearly

defined roles—specifically, who is speaking with the news media and how information will be shared. There need to be clear processes in place, including predeveloped scripts and communication command center guidelines. Also, many school districts will have mock drills that will help key players fine-tune their communication strategy and identify problems and gaps early.
- *Collaborative communication.* Most school districts have communication plans, but what about emergency services? In many cases, communication plans are specific to the organization—which creates silos. In a time of crisis, think about how many organizations will be involved—especially if the crisis occurs in a school. Let's count: you have the school district, local police or sheriff, fire department, and other emergency responders. If any of them are local, a good strategy would be to develop a collective emergency communication plan with clearly defined roles and who is communicating what. The community needs one message, not several mixed messages that can easily happen when there are multiple organizations or agencies involved. Think about creating a collaborative communication plan that is used by all organizations and agencies that will likely be involved in the event of a crisis or tragedy.
- *Keep calm.* When a crisis or tragedy occurs, the community quickly needs the board of education and superintendent to exhibit a calm, united, and clear message. Messages need to be carefully vetted, from one spokesperson, and convey a message of calm. If the superintendent or the board conveys a message of hysteria or confusion, the community will only become more excited, scared, and chaotic. Everyone in the community will want to carry the message, but the board of education and superintendent are responsible to deliver an accurate, timely, and sensitive message. They have this key responsibility.

KEY TAKEAWAY

Our hope is that no school board or superintendent will ever have to deal with a tragedy or crisis; however, in today's society, unfortunately, it appears every district will have to do so at some point in time. Boards of education and superintendents can never be too prepared. No matter how prepared a school board or superintendent is to address a situation, there will likely be mistakes or gaps. No organization is perfect.

But, the number of mistakes and gaps can be drastically reduced by taking preparation seriously. Have a plan that captures the needs of the district and clearly defined roles for everyone who is involved. Also, as communication plans are developed for tragedies, consider involving local law enforcement and emergency management services in developing a collaborative plan to reduce overlaps and gaps in messages.

Chapter Fourteen

Mistakes Happen, and How We Acknowledge Them Matters

Board of Education

Oops!

Superintendent

Mistakes are life's way of proving that we are human. Leaders who come to grips with mistakes and are transparent when things go wrong will earn an extra measure of credibility for their work.

When we think of the greatest organizations in the world—Apple and Facebook, Ford and Toyota, the Chicago Bulls and the New York Yankees—one constant among each of the mentioned teams is that they make mistakes regularly. Phone glitches. Fake political ads. Vehicle recalls. Championship game playoff losses.

All teams make mistakes, period. Boards of education and superintendents will make mistakes. There will be times when information is mistakenly released at the wrong time; information is not shared in a timely manner with the board, the superintendent, or the general public; or information is not clear, which only leads to confusion among stakeholders. No matter the mistake, as mentioned earlier, a timely response is needed.

Every organization is going to make a mistake. President Theodore Roosevelt said, "the only man who never makes a mistake is the man who never does anything." The worse thing that a board of education and superintendent could do is to not communicate out of fear of making a mistake. Too many organizations, public and private, focus on the possibility of mistakes, instead of focusing on the possibilities of the all the positives from doing!

To be clear, we are saying don't fear mistakes, only fear that *not* admitting or recognizing mistakes will occur. One of the worst things a board of education and superintendent can do is pretend that they are free from mistakes and that all of their decisions are without errors. There is no better way to alienate the general public than to pretend that the board of education and superintendent do not make mistakes.

Effective leaders own mistakes, while they recognize others for any success. Board members and the superintendent are ultimately where the "buck stops," like President Harry Truman said. Board teams are the governing board for the district, and the superintendent ensures that day-to-day operations run effectively, based on board policies. School districts are complex, as we continue to stress, with hundreds—if not thousands—of policies, statutes, and regulations that must be followed each day. The chance for mistakes to happen is extremely high. Understanding the complexities that come with running a school district helps boards of education and superintendents recognize that mistakes will undoubtedly occur.

Effective teams are quick to identify mistakes, share mistakes with pertinent people, and focus on addressing mistakes, not pointing fingers. Communication among the board and the superintendent is critical to creating a culture where mistakes are embraced, shared, and addressed quickly. Mistakes provide an excellent opportunity for boards of education and superintendents to collaborate to identify any revisions needed to board policies or procedures, identify organizational changes that need to occur, and identify needed communication strategies to keep the general public informed.

There is really nothing more powerful than a leader who admits mistakes and never takes credit for any success. We all appreciate leaders who exhibit humility, while we at the same time are turned off by those who do not. Communication again helps to instill a positive team culture focused on "we" and not "me." This is not easy because, naturally, the first inclination for many is to point fingers, disassociate from having anything to do with failure, or say, "I told you so."

High-performing boards of education and superintendents, however, have created such a team culture that communicating to the general public anything other than team acceptance of the mistake with strategies to avoid mistakes in the future is uncharacteristically abnormal. High-performing boards and superintendents are quick to respond to mistakes, own mistakes, and utilize mistakes to move the district forward.

Mistakes will assuredly happen—no matter the precautions the board of education and superintendent take to prevent them from occurring. We stress that mistakes will happen so that boards of education and superintendents recognize the need to develop a communication strategy that can be quickly used to communicate information to the general public. Furthermore, we stress mistakes happen so that boards of education and the superintendent can work diligently to create a team culture where mistakes are used to strengthen the team and district.

But creating a positive team culture, again, requires open, transparent, and frequent communication among board members and the superintendent so that trust helps forge the bonds necessary, where mistakes and successes are owned by the team, not any one board member or the superintendent. Remember, for anything positive to happen in the district, the board of education and superintendent must work toward the same vision.

PRACTICAL STRATEGIES

- *Own mistakes.* No matter the mistake, boards of education and superintendents must quickly own the mistake and communicate how the mistake will be corrected. Don't be afraid to communicate a message quickly. The key is to have a well-developed communication strategy where boards of education and superintendents can quickly respond to issues that may arise. But stay away from pointing fingers—though the press and general public will ask, the goal and task is to get people focused on the next steps going forward—focus on the horizon, not the past.
- *Develop and implement a communication strategy.* High-performing boards of education, superintendents, and school districts have a communication strategy that they use daily. Those teams have prewritten press releases ready to send out once information is updated and specifics are included. As mentioned earlier, a timely reply to any issue helps keep stakeholders' attention on the important work occurring. Also, it keeps stakeholders from losing trust in the team, the board of education, and the superintendent. Timely release of information is key to transparency. You cannot be transparent if someone releases the information before you do.
- *Harness the opportunity.* No matter the level of the mistake, there is an opportunity to turn a negative into a positive. Communicating next steps

not only helps keep the board of education and superintendent focused but also keeps the general public focused as well. While mistakes sometimes lead to confusion and restlessness, communicating how the district will be better due to this life lesson helps stakeholders focus more on what is to come, instead of focusing on the mistake that occurred. The general public is, for the most part, forgiving if they think leaders are upfront, honest, and transparent with information. As a reminder, every leader who has not been forthcoming with information has never succeeded or been effective. Share what you can, determined by your state's laws, and continue to move the district forward.

KEY TAKEAWAY

Members of the board of education and the superintendent can go from good to great by recognizing that mistakes must be shared, just like any successes. Though in many of today's organizational cultures there is a tendency to point fingers as a means to climb the career ladder, this really is a culture killer. Boards of education and superintendents must set the tone in the district where mistakes are quickly addressed, shared with others, and used as a means to advance the district.

Chapter Fifteen

Crafting a Year-Round School Communications Calendar

Board of Education

Communication Success Calendar			
Jan	Feb	Mar	Apr
May	Jun	Jul	Aug
Sep	Oct	Nov	Dec

Superintendent

Schools and districts have all sorts of good news stories that can pop up throughout the class year. Leaders can create a schedule by which public attention can be garnered by piggybacking on observations related to education.

OK, a show of hands, please. How many of you know of a positive occurrence or ongoing element of your district or individual school that you wish the community was aware of? If you aren't raising a hand—or two— wow, you must be a leader in a school system with a flat-out incredible, beyond-the-norm process of letting your target audiences know what's going on in your buildings. However, should you be one of those who acknowledged there are opportunities to shine the spotlight on student and staff sensations, there is an easy, no-expense tool to improve the chances of making it happen the next time around.

It's a simple item hanging in most offices or on kitchen refrigerators to remind us of important upcoming events from a birthday or anniversary to a trip to the dentist or an appointment to have the car serviced—a calendar. But this calendar is filled with a year's worth of reminders of annual observations that can be used to celebrate something about children, families, schools, and/or public education. And each occasion can be a chance to tag on with a nugget of positivity regarding your school system.

BUILDING THE LIST

While there are publications devoted to school observances that can be purchased from many outlets, a little time spent doing Google searches can produce a most satisfactory list of options. For example, in the month of August, the most obvious education-related event is—drum roll, please—the start of the new school year. It's a time of widespread public—and news media—attention to the return of students. And it's a great time to be spreading the word about new offerings, from academic subject matter and classroom technology to enhanced building security and safer transportation via the twice-daily bus routes.

But did you know that August has these observations?

- Get Ready for Kindergarten Month
- Children's Eye Health and Safety Month
- Immunization Awareness Month
- Wellness Month
- Crayon Collection Month
- Water Quality Month
- Truancy Prevention Month, Pedestrian Safety Month, and Artist Appreciation Month

September includes the following options:

- Childhood Injury Prevention Week
- Suicide Prevention Week
- Keep Kids Creative Week

- Security Officer Week
- Farm Safety and Health Week
- Backpack Safety Month
- College Savings Month
- Constitution Week
- Fruits and Veggies Month
- Emergency Preparedness Month
- National Hispanic Heritage Month

And October explodes with school-related observations that no one needs to stretch to tie in:

- Child Health Month
- Computer Learning Month
- Diversity Awareness Month
- Head Start Awareness Month
- Walk to School Month
- Arts and Humanities Month
- Bullying Prevention Month
- Field Trip Month
- School Bus Safety Week
- Red Ribbon Week (drug abuse awareness)
- Book Month, Earth Science and Chemistry Weeks, World Teacher Day, and much more

That's just the first three months of the school year!

We won't try to build such a calendar for readers, but one November observation bears special merit—American Education Week (AEW). AEW usually takes place the week before Thanksgiving, with a history that dates to 1921. Some school leaders may be reluctant to make a big deal out of AEW because of its connection and direction by the nation's largest teachers' union, the National Education Association.

But they may not note that among the many cosponsors of AEW are the American Association of School Administrators/The Superintendents Association, the National School Boards Association, the National PTA and organizations representing elementary and secondary principals and school counselors, and the American Legion. In short, AEW should be a celebratory week shared by school leaders at every level. With all the outside forces working against public education, school districts and school boards across the country should all celebrate American Education Week.

MAKING THE PITCH, SETTING THE HOOK

In public relations parlance, "setting the hook" simply means finding a way to pitch an idea, a message, or a story to a target audience (parents, general public, news media) in order to get their attention. So, the challenge for school leaders is to link the kind of observations noted earlier as well as local school success stories. The goal is engagement—not only reading about current events but also getting stakeholders like parents, guardians, grandparents, business leaders, and legislators in schools while also keeping constituents informed.

Some occasions are no-brainers like celebrating people (School Board Recognition Month in January, Teacher Appreciation Week in May, Principals Month in October, and Education Support Professionals Day in November) or education issues (Mathematics Awareness Month and School Volunteer Week in April, Summer Learning Week in July, and Health Education Month in October).

A special example comes around every spring—high school graduation. So here's a great tip to marry calendar and data. Have your high school counselors tabulate the total of college scholarship dollars that are being awarded to this year's graduating class. For a small district, this still can amount to tens of thousands of dollars; for a district with multiple high schools and/or a large senior class, the dollar amount can be several hundreds of thousands of dollars. Issue a press release. Report on this at the board meeting. Make mention of it at the commencement ceremony. Clearly, this is a message of the success of those graduating students gained through the work of dedicated teachers and supported by a school and district maximizing its means to help learners move to the next level of their education.

Other celebrations may take a little more creativity. But it's really no stretch to tie expanded dual credit options to College Readiness Month, new classroom software to Computer Learning Month, and additional preschool programming to Get Ready for Kindergarten Month. It just takes a little planning, willingness to seize an opportunity, and effort in looking for ways to use your new education events calendar as a "hook" to capture the interest of a desired segment of the school community.

PRACTICAL STRATEGIES

- *Board meetings.* As we noted in chapter 5, the meeting of the local board of education should be one forum for acknowledging what's taking place in the district and its schools. So, this option should be considered low-hanging fruit, creating at least a dozen times during each year for event-related salutes to staff and students involved in the good news. And it's an

excellent way to put student demonstrations of learning front and center before an audience almost exclusively focused on education issues.
- *Civic group meetings.* Community groups like Rotary, Lions and Optimist clubs, Chambers of Commerce, PTAs, and retired teacher chapters have at least one thing in common—when they meet, they like to have a presentation. And every group that has regular presentations has some poor soul serving as the program chairperson. It's a good idea for school systems to keep track of these desperate volunteers who, anywhere from quarterly to monthly, must come up with a topical session of interest to their members. Pitching a school program in March, for example, could be tied to National Reading Month and a program on efforts of the district to boost students' literacy skills.
- *Newspaper letters to the editor.* Yes, newspaper readership numbers are declining, but online newspaper engagement is trending in the other direction. And in both forums, one element of newspapers that remains almost universal is the letter to the editor section. Superintendents and boards already should be taking advantage of this opinion venue when they need to educate the public on major issues. But a letter to the editor also can be used to boost reader attention to matters like motorists' responsibilities with an item during School Bus Safety Week in October.
- *Social media posts.* Daily school and district Facebook and Twitter posts are perfect platforms for delivering calendar-related tidbits about good things going on involving students and learning. Even with the 140-character limit for a tweet, the observation-linked communication is practical. It only takes 21 characters to tie in "security officer week" to a post about the value of school resource officers patrolling school hallways, interacting with students, and ensuring they have a safe place to learn.
- *Annual district magazine.* Many districts have discovered how powerful the annual district magazine can be for informing stakeholders while also building the district's brand. Different from the monthly newsletter or bulletin, the annual district magazine is the district's opportunity to showcase all the great things that happened throughout the school year and to introduce the public to the new school year. Many districts refer to this as the "District's Yearbook" because there are numerous photos of students, staff, leaders, board members, and community partners.

KEY TAKEAWAY

Creating a year-round list of education observations establishes an added resource for superintendents and school board members wishing to heighten public awareness of those local success stories that may not garner front page news or even much more than a paragraph in a monthly newsletter. Yet they also represent an ongoing supply of possibilities—large and small—where leaders can share positive narratives with those audiences who pay the taxes, accomplish the tasks, and supply the vital elements of education—their children—needed to make public education work in your communities.

Conclusion
A Final Thought

Creating a *maximum impact* in a school district requires a board of education and superintendent that understand the importance of communication. More important, boards of education and superintendents must be able to effectively communicate their vision. As we have conveyed throughout this book, effective communication begins with a clear team vision for the school district. Legendary basketball coach Mike Krzyzewski says, "Effective teamwork begins and ends with communication."

Communication requires a team approach that begins with trust and always ends with transparency. There is nothing more effective than a team that has a culture of trust and transparency. Today's schools, across the nation, need school boards and superintendents who have forged a team based on a clear vision and transparency. By focusing on a unifying purpose and openness, the board and superintendent are better positioned to communicate as a team.

As public dissatisfaction toward public education continues to increase, school boards and superintendents must begin to communicate in a clear, concise, and unified message. High-performing teams value everyone's views, voices, and perspectives yet collaboratively communicate via one voice. They do so by empowering each team member to voice their concerns and priorities but instill the belief and expectation of team consensus. Members of a high-performing team recognize that they may not get everything that they want but also that the effectiveness of the team is paramount over the needs of the individual.

No school board and superintendent will have a maximum impact without a communication strategy. As a team, they must first establish expectations and roles when communicating a team message. Too often, too many members of the board and the superintendent communicate as individual team members and not as a team. Those boards and superintendents never really form a team that will lead to sustainable success for the district or for students. Discombobulated or sporadic messages are usually functions of an ineffective team. Sadly, mixed messages, incomplete information, and lack of transparency by boards of education and the superintendent has led to the negative views toward public education today.

Communication can change the conversation for public education. There must be a movement in every district across the nation to focus on communication strategy. Boards of education and superintendents must be the leaders who establish the expectations for the district, including the communication strategy. Public education must remove distrust, by communicating more succinctly and consistently about the many successes that are occurring each day. But just as important, boards of education and superintendents must also not be afraid to communicate and talk about mistakes and what changes need to occur. Be honest and unafraid to say change must happen—clearly, compassionately, and as a team.

The success of the district, the organization, and the team depends on the ability of the board of education and superintendent to communicate. Keep in mind that, as with everything else, you must choose quality over quantity. Too much communication, without really sharing pertinent information, is worse than not communicating at all.

Boards of education and superintendents must be strategic in their approach to communicating not only the vision for the district but also the district's goals, successes, and information. Communicate what stakeholders need to know, what they want to know, and what they will value. To have a *maximum impact* in the district, weighing the importance of information shared and conveyed by the board of education and superintendent, as a team, is precisely what is needed in today's school district.

Afterword
Putting Maximum Impact *into Action*

This book offers a compelling call to action that communication has never been more important for public schools, and that communication must be a central pillar of governance and leadership of the board/superintendent team. To chart your next steps, I urge boards to consider the topics raised in this book from a governing lens: as in all issues, your most powerful levers for change are policy, planning, resource allocation, and your own leadership skills.

Policy: Review your board policies relating to school/community relations and the topics of this book. Board policies can clarify your intent and practices on issues such as purposes of a communications program, news media relations, social media guidelines, public participation at board meetings, and more. The discussions your board has in policy development and review can strengthen commitment and understanding of the team, as well as set the tone for staff and community that these issues are important to you.

Strategic Planning: It is very hard to communicate strategy when you don't have one, or to build a brand around a vague notion of who you are as a district. A meaningful strategic planning process can bring the board team, staff, and community together in building momentum toward the "forward focus on growth" the authors urge in chapter 7. Sound planning processes can help your board consider how societal trends impact student needs, understand community priorities and values, and build unity among stakeholders on priorities to move forward.

Resource Allocation: Assess the level of personnel and operational budgetary resources allocated to communications in your district. Superintendents may play an active role, as the authors urge, but their efforts should be supported by designated staff responsibility and budgetary resources allocated to communications. Professional communication staffing is ideal, but adding staff may not be feasible in all districts given today's budget climate. If your district uses educational or support staff for certain communications functions such as maintaining a district website, ensure those staff have the professional development needed for success.

Board Learning: Discuss your own knowledge and skill to identify a plan for board development on issues raised in *Maximum Impact*. What are your current strengths? Where are gaps in knowledge and skill? Consider seeking board development on media spokesperson skills, legal and free speech issues related to social media, or practices of the board to support "one voice" principles. Learn from your peers by seeking out sessions at conferences where other board/superintendent teams profile their communications efforts.

Your state school boards association can help your board take its next steps to achieve *Maximum Impact* in your communications efforts with sample policies, planning and goal-setting facilitation, consulting, and board development opportunities. In addition, the National School Public Relations Association (NSPRA) and state NSPRA chapters offer important supports for communications efforts.

The key is getting started on the next steps for your own maximum impact as a board!

Lisa Bartusek
Former Associate Executive Director,
National School Boards Association
Former National Chairperson of Council of
School Boards Association Communicators

Index

About the Authors

Brian Creasman, EdD, is currently superintendent of Fleming County Schools in Kentucky. He is the 2020 Kentucky Superintendent of the Year. His Twitter account says he has the best job in Kentucky. He has served as an assistant superintendent, a high school and middle school principal and assistant principal, and an instructional technologist and classroom teacher. He is the coauthor of *The Leader Within: Understanding and Empowering Teacher Leaders*; *Growing Leaders Within: A Process toward Teacher Leadership*; *Can Every School Succeed? Bending Constructs to Transform an American Icon*; and *ConnectED Leaders: Network and Amplify Your Superintendency*. Brian can be reached at briankcreasman@gmail.com. He can also be found on Twitter at @FCSSuper. He is the comoderator of #bendingED, the national and international school transformation chat on Twitter.

Brad Hughes manages an education news Twitter blog (@gymobrad), which attracts more than 22,000 engagements daily. He worked 44 years as a print and broadcast journalist, public affairs and social media director, and spokesman for Kentucky state government and the Kentucky School Boards Association. For more than two decades, he wrote magazine columns on education communications for the *Kentucky School Advocate*, the *American School Board Journal*, and the *School Administrator*. His communications training for school leaders has taken him to 27 states and Canada. Hughes has been honored by the National School Boards Association, the National Association for Year-Round Education, the Bluegrass Society of Professional Journalists, the Kentucky School Public Relations Association, and the Council of School Board Association Communicators.

www.ingramcontent.com/pod-product-compliance
Lightning Source LLC
Chambersburg PA
CBHW070735230426
43665CB00016B/2247